Southern Menus

for

Entertaining

By

William E. Coxwell

cookbooks
by morris press
P.O. Box 2110 · Kearney, NE 68848

Dedication

This book is dedicated to
Mother,
Geneva H. Coxwell,
who taught me the aesthetics of
cooking and instilled in me her philosophy:
"simplicity is elegance".

and

In memory of the "Cheese Straw Lady",
Mrs. Fan Story
for sharing her cheese straw recipe and for
teaching me that laughter is the most
important ingredient in Southern cooking.

Fan's Original Cheese Straws

Yield: 6 dozen

16 ounces New York extra sharp cheddar cheese
1 1/2 sticks butter *(NO margarine)*
1 teaspoon salt
1 teaspoon baking powder
1 1/2 teaspoons cayenne pepper
2 cups plain all-purpose flour

1. Grate cheese and place in a large mixing bowl.
2. Place butter sticks on top of cheese and cover with plastic wrap.
3. Let stand overnight to reach room temperature.
4. Add other ingredients.
5. Knead thoroughly with hands until well mixed and a large ball is formed.
6. Pipe through a cookie press onto greased baking sheets.
7. Bake at 400° for 8-10 minutes, watching closely so straws don't burn.
8. They should be <u>barely</u> brown around edges.
9. Cut into pieces while warm.
10. Place in airtight tins and freeze or refrigerate.

Note: This recipe doubles easily and freezes well. I do not recommend freezing for longer than three months. For hotter straws use more cayenne.

Mother's Pear Preserves

Yield: 10-12 pints

1 peck fresh pears
5 pounds granulated sugar
1 teaspoon salt
12 pint jars with rings and seals

1. Wash pears; peel and quarter, discarding seed and core.
2. Place in a large enamel pot or dish pan.
3. Pour sugar over fruit covering well.
4. Cover and let stand overnight.
5. Stir well; begin cooking, <u>uncovered</u>, over medium heat, stirring often.
6. After sugar is melted and fruit begins to boil, reduce heat to medium low.
7. Stir often to prevent sticking and scorching.
8. Continue stirring often and cooking for several hours until syrup reaches a desired consistency.
9. Pour into hot sterilized jars and seal.
10. Store when cooled completely.

Note: The author prefers the preserves when they reach a coppery-golden color. While still warm they are delicious over vanilla ice cream.

Definition:

Peck- 8 quarts.

Of Kitchens and Lessons Learned

It was a cramped cluttered little kitchen. Marbled, faded jade green counter tops, very reminiscent of the 1960's were covered with various cooking paraphernalia. Walls and cabinets were pine paneling with dark oval knots like black eyes that stared blank. The floor was bland linoleum. That was the kitchen of my childhood home in the quiet neighborhood on Pineview Drive.

It was where the beginning of my culinary career took place. My early experiments were made manifest in small cakes that did not rise but bounced; of Jell-O that would not congeal and hard miniature mounds that I called biscuits. I did not become discouraged! I watched daddy peel and cut vegetables, fry chicken, make corn muffins and wash the dishes. Field trips were to the grocery store and produce stands. Daddy's kitchen management was meticulous; he took pride in finding bargains.

Mother also used that small spice scented workshop. She baked the cakes, pies, puddings and cobblers and made her fudge and divinity as menus dictated. That was where the true fun was: mixing bowls lined with sweet creamy batter, pots encrusted with excruciatingly sweet fudge residue and beaters frosted with thick sticky icing. During those early stages I learned by watching, tasting and remembering as much as possible. The kitchen was my first playground.

In South Carolina there were other kitchens, new sights and more wondrous smells. There was the hot stuffy little box kitchen where Uncle Bill's cook, Mate, baked her delicate little biscuits in aged coal black baking pans. Mama Kate's kitchen had it perpetual scent of fried chicken and yeast rolls. Her table was always immaculately set with her Desert Rose china and cut glass dishes filled with homemade pickles and relishes made with vegetables harvested from her garden. She was a thrifty homemaker and saved vegetable peelings for the compost heap. That was my first encounter with the term "compost bed" and the prolific use of leftovers.

My sister, Mary, had a kitchen on a far grander scale than I was accustomed. Her counter tops were an unoccupied sea of workspace. Her foods were different, well made creations that expanded my palate. Mary's kitchen gave my sense of taste its personality. That is why I return to memories of her cooking style again and again.

As I gained experience and became more agile in "food works", I would spend long hours with my dear friend, Nana, cooking, eating, and cleaning. One of my most cherished memories is preparing her home and cooking dinner for her Bridge Club Christmas party. It was great fun!

Eventually, I took over the cramped, cluttered kitchen on Pineview Drive, revamped its debris strewn work surfaces and began my own catering business. I learned innovative storage and preparation techniques, usually the hard way, after near disasters. I discovered the best way to learn is by experience, through trial and error. Cooking can be not only a career or a hobby but also a form of therapy. Kitchens were places where I continually learned and they are an important part of my childhood memories.

As I gained momentum and became more confident in my abilities, I decided to open a restaurant in a beautifully restored old home. It was an exciting time. It was a learning time. As the business grew I expanded to using two kitchens, one for hot foods and one for cold foods, departmentalizing for efficiency. That was where I truly began to explore and experience the world of food. I continue to visit kitchens and rummage through pantries. I enjoy watching others in their craft and enhancing my culinary skills. The world of food and kitchens is multifaceted and is endless in how it affects each of us. Learning never ends.

Introduction

The South is a pretty world filled with fragrant magnolias and gray ghosts of Spanish moss; a land strewn with ribbons of rivers and peppered with plantations. It embodies tradition-lax Sunday lunches, heirloom silver, and first cousins twice removed. It is all things polished and proud, simple and elegant. Southerners pride themselves on their hospitality and the ease with which they entertain. Full tables miraculously seat one more and the unexpected company finds a delicious meal waiting.

The South has a style of hospitality, entertaining simply and elegantly with a quiet charm and grace. There is a code, time-honored in the South, to do all things with a generous hand, yet simply, extending it with the utmost kindness and sincerity. Southerners have turned entertaining into an art.

The South is my home and I cherish the traditions that filled and surrounded my childhood. I have attempted to arrange a collection of recipes that will benefit both the novice and experienced cook. Also included are a few reminiscences that I hope will help demonstrate how vital food is to our emotional and physical needs. Food also plays an important part in our social development. It is comforting. It is a form of security.

Moods of food change with times and seasons. I have arranged seasonal menus of a wide variety but many of the foods are interchangeable, creating a myriad of menus. There is also a "Basics Section" with recipes that will be used repeatedly. I have also included information on stock making and perfecting pie dough, as well as an herb-spice guide and an all-purpose glossary. I have exerted every effort to make this book as informative and interesting as possible to encourage you on your culinary venture. Happy Cooking!

- William Coxwell

Table Of Contents

The Season of Spring

Menus for Spring

A Luncheon for the Bride

Garden Club Brunch

Easter Sunday Lunch

A Special Luncheon
for Mother

Light Spring Supper

A Luncheon for the Bride

Marianne's Gourmet Chicken Salad

Joanne's Apricot Salad

Fresh Seasonal Fruit

Angel Biscuits
(Bill's Basics p.206)

Lemon Chess Pie

Marianne's Gourmet Chicken Salad

Yield: 8 servings

4 chicken breasts
1 cup sliced green seedless grapes
2 Tablespoons minced parsley
1/4 teaspoon dill weed
1 cup finely diced celery
1/2 cup toasted pecan halves
1/2 cup half and half
1 cup mayonnaise
salt and black pepper to taste

1. Cook chicken breasts in salted water.
2. Drain, cool and debone breasts.
3. Cut into bite size pieces.
4. Mix with remaining ingredients and adjust seasoning with salt and pepper to taste.
5. Chill well before serving.

*Note: To serve arrange on a bed of green leaf lettuce or curly endive leaves and garnish with a small cluster of green grapes.

Joanne's Apricot Salad

Yield: 12 servings

6 ounces orange Jell-O
2 cups boiling water
1 cup miniature marshmallows
16 ounce can apricot halves in syrup
10 ounces Cool Whip, divided
1/2 cup shredded cheddar cheese

1. Dissolve Jell-O and marshmallows in boiling water.
2. Add the **juice** from the can of apricots.
3. Refrigerate until firm.
4. Combine 1/4 cup Cool Whip, can of apricots and congealed mixture in the bowl of a food processor or blender.
5. Puree until smooth. *(May have to do in two batches).*
6. Pour into a 9 1/2 x 13 inch pyrex dish and refrigerate until firm.
7. Top with remaining Cool Whip.
8. Sprinkle with cheese.
9. Serve on a lettuce leaf.

Lemon Chess Pie

Yield: 8 servings

1 9-inch deep dish pie shell
1/2 cup butter, softened
2 cups sugar
5 eggs
juice of 3 lemons
grated zest of 3 lemons
3 Tablespoons all-purpose flour
confectioner's sugar for dusting

1. Cream butter and sugar.
2. Add eggs and beat well.
3. Add lemon juice, zest and flour, mixing well.
4. Pour filling into pie shell and bake at 300° for 30-45 minutes or until pie is set and top is golden brown.
5. Cool completely.
6. Sprinkle top with confectioner's sugar if desired.

Garden Club Brunch

Fan's Breakfast Casserole

Dianne Wood's Creamy Grits

Sister's Blueberry Muffins

Fresh Fruit in a Grapefruit Bowl

Angel Biscuits
(Bill's Basics p.)

Mother's Pear Preserves
(Dedication p.2)

Fan's Breakfast Casserole

Yield: 6-8 servings

1 pound bulk sausage (hot)
8 ounce can crescent roll dough
1 cup mozzarella cheese, shredded
1 cup cheddar cheese, shredded
4 large eggs
1 cup milk
1/4 teaspoon salt
1/8 teaspoon black pepper

1. Brown sausage and drain.
2. Spray a 9 x 13-inch Pyrex dish with cooking spray and layer with the crescent dough.
3. Press perforated edges together to seal and form a crust.
4. Sprinkle with sausage, then cheeses in order listed.
5. Whisk eggs, milk, salt and pepper together.
6. Pour egg mixture over sausage/cheese.
7. Bake at 400° for 25-30 minutes or until light brown and puffy.

Note: If your oven tends to cook "hot" reduce the temperature 5 to 10 degrees and extend the cooking time 10 minutes.

Dianne Wood's
Creamy Grits

Yield: 4-6 servings

1 cup Quick Grits
4 cups water
salt to taste
1/2 stick margarine

1. Bring water to boil in a large pot.
2. Add salt.
3. Add grits and stir.
4. Turn down the temperature to low.
5. Cook the grits at low temperature for 2 hours.
6. Add margarine and stir just before serving.

Sister's Blueberry Muffins

Yield: 24 muffins

3 cups all-purpose flour
1 cup sugar plus 2 Tablespoons
4 teaspoons baking powder
1 teaspoon salt
1 cup milk
2 cups blueberries (fresh or frozen)
1/2 cup oil
1 egg

1. Sift flour, sugar, baking powder and salt.
2. Mix milk, oil and egg.
3. Make a well in the center of the dry ingredients and pour the liquid mixture into the well.
4. Stir until blended. **Do not over mix!**
5. Fold in blueberries.
6. Spoon batter into well greased muffin tins or paper lined muffin tins and bake at 400° for 20-25 minutes or until toothpick inserted comes out clean.

Fresh Fruit
in a Grapefruit Bowl

Yield: 6 servings

3 large grapefruits, halved and seeds removed
1 papaya, halved and seeds removed
2 oranges, peeled and cut into wedges
1 pint fresh raspberries or strawberries, hulls
  removed
Grand Marnier to taste (orange-flavored liqueur)
fresh sprigs of mint

1. Scoop out grapefruit halves, eliminating any
   pith and membrane; set aside.
2. Be sure orange wedges are minus any pith
   and membrane.
3. Gently toss all fruits in a glass bowl.
4. The bottoms of the grapefruit may need
   trimming so that they will be level and not
   topple over when served.
5. Spoon fruit mixture into the grapefruit half.
6. Drizzle each fruit bowl with a little Grand
   Marnier, if desired.
7. Garnish with a sprig of fresh mint.

*Note: If you prefer to omit the alcohol, mix a small amount of orange
juice with confectioner's sugar to form a thin glaze and use in
place of the liqueur.*

Easter Sunday Lunch

Blueberry Congealed Salad

Bourbon Glazed Baked Ham

Fresh Corn-Frozen Corn

Mother's Candied Sweet Potatoes

Fresh Green Beans

Yeast Rolls

Praline Cake

Blueberry Congealed Salad

Yield: 12 servings

6 ounce package raspberry Jell-O
2 cups grape juice (not white)
1 can blueberry pie filling
1 20 ounce can crushed pineapple, drained
8 ounces cream cheese, softened
1 cup sour cream
1/2 cup sugar
1/2 teaspoon vanilla
1 cup pecans, finely chopped

1. Heat grape juice and dissolve Jell-O.
2. Add crushed pineapple and pie filling
3. Pour into a 9 1/2 x 13-inch pyrex dish and chill until firm.
4. Cream together cream cheese sour cream and sugar until fluffy.
5. Spread cream cheese mixture over congealed mixture.
6. Sprinkle with finely chopped pecans.

Bourbon Glazed Baked Ham

Yield: 8-10 servings

1 ham, butt portion, partially cooked
brown sugar
bourbon

1. Bake ham in a brown paper bag at 325° for 20 minutes per pound.
2. Mix equal parts of brown sugar and bourbon to form a thick glaze.
3. Increase oven heat to 375°.
4. Spoon some of the glaze over the ham and return to the oven for 5-10 minutes.
5. Repeat until all glaze is used and ham is a deep red-brown color.

Fresh Green Beans

Yield: 6 servings

3 pounds fresh green beans
3 slices bacon
water
2 teaspoons sugar

1. Snip ends off green beans and snap into bite size pieces.
2. With enough water to keep beans from sticking to the bottom of the pan, cook the bacon about 10-15 minutes.
   (If using a ham hock, boil until done.)
3. Add beans and cook covered over a medium heat, adding water as needed.
4. Cook until desired doneness.
5. When beans are almost done, sprinkle with sugar.
6. Taste and add extra salt and pepper if desired.

Fresh Corn-Frozen Corn

Yield: 6 servings

16 ounces frozen whole kernel corn
whole milk as needed
salt to taste
black pepper to taste
3 Tablespoons all-purpose flour
3 Tablespoons sugar
1 stick of margarine, melted

1. Put corn in large sauce pan and cover with milk.
2. Season with salt (about 1 teaspoon)
3. Cook on low heat until corn is tender.
4. When corn is tender, drain off 2/3 of the milk.
5. Add flour, sugar, margarine, and pepper.
6. Allow corn to cool about 10 minutes.
7. Put through a food processor or food mill until partially pureed.*
8. Some kernels should be left whole for texture to be correct.
9. Return to stove and cook on low heat until thickened.
10. Taste and adjust seasonings.

Note: A hand held blender, if you own one, is excellent for this process; easier-faster-and less clean up!

Mother's Candied Sweet Potatoes

Yield: 6-8 servings

1 cup sugar
3/4 cup water
1/4 teaspoon salt
1/2 cup butter
2 large red sweet potatoes
1/2 cup white Karo corn syrup
1 teaspoon vanilla flavoring

1. Peel sweet potatoes and cut into strips.
2. Mix all other ingredients in a heavy skillet and heat to boiling, over low heat.
3. Drop the potato strips into the boiling mixture.
4. Cook uncovered, slowly for 1 to 1 1/2 hours.
5. Shake pan frequently, to prevent potatoes from sticking.

Yeast Rolls

Yield: 7-8 dozen

2 each 1/4 ounce envelopes yeast
1 cup lukewarm water
1 cup sugar
1 cup Crisco
1 cup water
2 eggs
6 cups all-purpose flour

1. Dissolve yeast in 1 cup lukewarm water and set aside.
2. In microwave, melt the Crisco and hot water; add sugar, stirring to dissolve.
3. Combine yeast water with Crisco-sugar water and add the eggs.
4. When liquid is well mixed, stir into 6 cups all-purpose flour.
5. Cover entire mixture with plastic wrap and refrigerate overnight.
6. For shaping and baking see "How to Make Parker House Rolls".

How to Make
Parker House Rolls

1. Roll out a portion of the dough to 1/4 inch thick on a lightly floured board or counter top.
2. Using a 2 inch round cutter, cut out circles.
3. Lightly spread half of the circle with softened margarine or butter.
4. Fold unbuttered side over onto buttered portion to form a semi circle.
5. Press down gently.
6. Place on a greased baking sheet.
7. Repeat using remaining dough or until you have prepared the desired number of rolls.
8. Refrigerate remaining dough for up to 24 hours.
9. Cover with a tea-towel or paper towel and let rest at room temperature for 1 1/2 to 2 hours.
10. Bake at 425° until lightly browned and puffy.
11. Brush with melted butter and serve hot.
12. Rolls can be frozen and served later-thawed in a single layer and reheated in aluminum foil.

Praline Cake

Yield: 15-18 servings

Cake:

1 stick oleo	2 eggs
1 cup hot buttermilk	2 cups all-purpose flour
2 cups brown sugar	1 Tablespoon cocoa
1 teaspoon baking soda	
1 teaspoon vanilla extract	

Topping:

1 stick oleo	1 teaspoon vanilla extract
1 cup flaked coconut	3/4 cup chopped pecans
1 cup brown sugar	
6 Tablespoons evaporated milk	

1. For cake, melt oleo in hot buttermilk.
2. Add sugar.
3. Beat in eggs and vanilla.
4. Add flour, baking soda and cocoa.
5. Stir well.
6. Turn into a greased 9 1/2 x 13 inch baking dish.
7. Bake at 350° for 20-30 minutes.
8. For topping, mix all ingredients well.
9. Spread over hot cake as soon as it is taken from oven.
10. Run under the broiler until bubbly and toasted.

Special Luncheon for Mother

Lime-Buttermilk Salad

Sunday Chicken Breasts

Oriental Rice

Asparagus with Lemon Butter

Betty Adams' Sour Cream
Pound Cake

Lemon Ice Cream

Lime-Buttermilk Salad

Yield: 12 servings

6 ounces lime Jell-O
16 ounce can crushed pineapple
2 cups buttermilk
8 ounces Cool Whip
1 cup chopped pecans

1. Place crushed pineapple and Jell-O into a small saucepan.
2. Heat, stirring constantly until Jell-O dissolves.
3. Whip buttermilk and Cool Whip together.
4. Fold into Jell-O mixture.
5. Pour into a 9 1/2 x 13 inch pyrex casserole.
6. Sprinkle chopped nuts over the top.
7. Chill until firm.

Sunday Chicken Breasts

Yield: 6 servings

6 boneless chicken breasts
6 slices uncooked bacon
6 sliced dried beef
1 can cream of mushroom soup
1 cup sour cream

1. Wrap each chicken breast with a slice of bacon.
2. Place each bacon wrapped breast on a slice of dried beef.
3. Place in a greased Pyrex casserole dish of appropriate size. *(I suggest an 8 x 8 inch size.)*
4. Combine soup and sour cream.
5. Spoon over breasts, being sure all are well covered.
6. Bake uncovered at 275° for 1 1/2 to 2 hours.
7. Do not let the bottoms burn.

Oriental Rice

Yield: 10 servings

4 cups cooked white rice
3/4 stick butter or margarine
1 large onion, chopped
1 large green bell pepper, chopped
1/2 cup sliced almonds
4 ounces chopped pimento (1 small jar)
1/4 cup soy sauce
1/2 cup sliced fresh mushrooms or one 4 ounce
    jar of sliced mushrooms, drained
1 teaspoon garlic powder

1. Melt butter in a large skillet.
2. Add onion, bell pepper and mushrooms.
3. Saute for 3-5 minutes until vegetables are tender.
4. Add saute mixture to cooked rice.
5. Add remaining ingredients to cooked rice and stir well.
6. Adjust seasonings carefully because soy sauce is salty.
7. Place into a greased casserole dish, cover and bake at 350° until heated through.

Asparagus
with Lemon Butter

Yield: 4-6 servings

2 bunches fresh asparagus
salted water
lemon pepper to taste
1 fresh lemon, sliced
1 stick butter, melted

1. Trim woody stems from asparagus.
2. Cook in salted water to cover until tender, but not overdone. This will vary depending upon size of asparagus spears.
3. Drain well and sprinkle with lemon pepper.
4. Place sliced lemons in a small skillet.
5. Add melted butter,
6. Cook for several minutes.
7. Spoon lemon butter over asparagus when ready to serve.
8. Garnish with a few slices of buttered lemon.

Betty Adams'
Sour Cream Pound Cake

Yield: 16 slices

1/2 cup Crisco
2 sticks margarine, softened
3 cups sugar
6 large eggs
3 1/2 cups cake flour
1 cup sour cream
1/4 teaspoon salt
1/4 teaspoon baking powder
1 teaspoon vanilla flavoring
1 teaspoon butter flavoring

1. Sift cake flour.
2. Remeasure and sift again, this time adding salt and baking powder; set aside.
3. Cream margarine, Crisco and sugar until smooth.
4. Add eggs, one at a time, beating well after each addition.
5. Add flour, alternating with sour cream.
6. Beat until fluffy.
7. Add vanilla and butter flavorings, beating well.
8. Pour into a greased and floured tube pan.
9. Bake at 325° for 1 1/2 hours.
10. Invert onto a plate and cool.

Lemon Ice Cream

Yield: 8-10 servings

1 cup lemon juice
4 cups sugar
3 pints whipping cream
rock salt and crushed ice for churning
sprigs of fresh mint to garnish

1. Whisk together lemon juice and sugar.
2. Add whipping cream.
3. Pour into the well of an ice cream churn.
4. Churn with lots of rock salt and ice according to directions specified for your churn.
5. Serve in a pretty dish and garnish with a sprig of mint.

Note: For added color I like to serve this sprinkled with a few fresh raspberries or blueberries.

Light Spring Supper

Caesar Salad

Apricot-Lemon Grilled Chicken

Baked Squash

Grilled Tomatoes

Wild Rice Casserole

Commercial French Bread

Lemon-Pecan Tart

Caesar Salad

Yield: 8-10 servings

2 heads romaine lettuce, torn
3/4 cup freshly grated Parmesan cheese
1 cup homemade or commercial croutons

Dressing:

1/4 cup lemon juice
1/4 cup red wine vinegar
3/4 cup olive oil
1 large anchovy fillet
pressed garlic to taste
black pepper to taste
dash Worcestershire
1 egg, slightly beaten

1. Place lettuce, cheese and croutons in a large salad bowl; toss gently.
2. Blend lemon juice, vinegar and olive oil together; set aside.
3. In a small bowl, mash the anchovy with a fork into a paste.
4. Add garlic, pepper, Worcestershire and egg.
5. Mix well and adjust seasonings.
6. Combine with lemon juice mixture.
7. Drizzle small amount over salad greens and toss to coat.
8. Repeat until desired flavor is achieved.

Apricot-Lemon Grilled Chicken

Yield: 6-8 servings

6-8 boneless chicken breasts
1 envelope french onion soup mix
1 18 ounce jar apricot preserves
2 lemons, sliced and seeds removed

1. Prick breasts with tines of fork and place in a pyrex or tupperware container.
2. Combine soup mix, apricot preserves and lemon slices.
3. Pour over chicken breasts, cover and chill overnight.
4. Prepare your grill according to manufacturer's directions.
5. Grill breasts over hot coals 12-15 minutes for average size breasts and 15-20 minutes for larger breasts.
6. Baste periodically with additional apricot mixture.

Baked Squash

Yield: 6 servings

6 medium size yellow summer squash *(crookneck)*
6 teaspoons butter or margarine, melted
fresh ground black pepper to taste
salt to taste

1. Wash squash thoroughly and trim ends.
2. Slice squash horizontally, creating 2 boat-like slices.
3. With the point of a sharp knife, make a few slits diagonally across the fruit of the squash, being careful not to pierce the skin.
4. Pour 1 teaspoon of melted butter over each squash slice.
5. Sprinkle with salt and black pepper.
6. Place on a foil lined and buttered baking sheet and bake at 350° 15-20 minutes until squash are tender.
7. Serve 2 slices of squash per person.

Grilled Tomatoes

Yield: 6 servings

3 firm ripe red tomatoes
2 Tablspoons olive oil
2 Tablespoons fresh minced herbs of choice
   (my favorites are basil, thyme, oregano and tarragon)
fresh ground black pepper to taste

1. Prepare grill according to manufacturer's directions.
2. With a sharp knife, carve out the stem end of the tomato; DO NOT CORE COMPLETELY.
3. Slice tomatoes in half horizontally and place slice side up on a baking sheet.
4. Drizzle with the olive oil and sprinkle with herbs and black pepper.
5. Place slice side down on the grill and grill 3-5 minutes until slightly tender and slightly charred.
6. Tomatoes may be sprinkled with more herbs before serving to enhance presentation if desired.

Wild Rice Casserole

Yield: 6 servings

1 cup wild rice, washed
water
6 Tablespoons butter or margarine
1 pound fresh mushrooms, sliced
3/4 cup sliced scallions *(white and green parts)*
salt to taste
1/4 teaspoon black pepper
1/2 cup sliced almonds
3 cups chicken broth
1 1/2 cups heavy cream or half & half
2 Tablespoons Gallo Sherry

1. Cover rice with water in a saucepan and bring to a boil.
2. Remove from heat and let stand 1 hour, then drain.
3. Melt 3 Tablespoons butter in a skillet.
4. Add mushrooms and scallions and saute until lightly browned.
5. In a large bowl, combine rice and all other ingredients.
6. Mix well and pour into a buttered 1 quart pyrex casserole dish.
7. Cover and bake at 350° for 1 1/4 hours.
8. Uncover and dot with remaining butter and bake an additional 10 minutes.

Note: A small can of sliced water chesnuts may be added if desired. Simply drain and add them to step 5.

Lemon-Pecan Tart

Yield: 8 slices

1 9-inch deep dish pie shell
4 eggs, slightly beaten
6 Tablespoons melted butter
grated zest of 1 lemon
3/4 cup Karo syrup *(light or dark)*
1/2 cup sugar
3 Tablespoons all-purpose flour
1/4 cup lemon juice
1 cup chopped pecans

1. Preheat oven to 350°.
2. Prick bottom of pie shell with tines of a fork.
3. Whisk all ingredients together except pecans and add them last.
4. Pour into pie shell and bake for 45 minutes to 1 hour or until filling is set.

*Note: To garnish slices, dust them lightly with confectioner's sugar and serve with a lemon twist.

The

Season

of

Summer

Menus for Summer

Southern Ice Cream Social

Canning and Preserving

Father's Day Picnic

July Fourth in Carolina

Southern Barbeque

Fancy Fish Dinner

Southern Ice Cream Social

Cherry Chocolate Chip Ice Cream

Blueberry Cheesecake Ice Cream

Banana-Walnut Ice Cream

White Chocolate Ice Cream

Robin Dudley's Straw-Ba-Nut Ice Cream

Cherry Chocolate Chip
Ice Cream

Yield: about 3 1/2 quarts

2 cans sweetened condensed milk
1 large can evaporated milk
6 ounces semi-sweet chocolate chips
7 ounce jar maraschino cherries
1 teaspoon almond extract
whole milk as needed
additional sugar to taste or as needed

1. Coarsely chop cherries in food processor with their juice.
2. Combine cherries with sweetened condensed milk, evaporated milk, chocolate chips, and almond extract.
3. Pour into the well of an ice cream churn and fill to the "fill line" with whole milk.
4. At this point add any additional sugar if desired.
5. Churn with lots of rock salt and ice according to manufacturer's directions for your churn.
6. Before serving, stir well to help distribute chips and cherries that may have settled during the churning process.

Blueberry Cheesecake

Ice Cream

Yield: about 4 quarts

8 ounces cream cheese, softened
2 cups confectioner's sugar
3 pints half & half
8 ounces Cool Whip
1 can blueberry pie filling
sugar to taste
whole milk as needed

1. Cream confectioner's sugar and cream cheese until smooth.
2. Combine with half & half and Cool Whip.
3. Pour into churn and fill to "fill line" with whole milk and sweeten to taste with addional sugar.
4. Add the can of blueberry pie filling on top.
5. The pie filling will be incorporated as the paddle churns the ice cream.
6. Churn with lots of rock salt and ice according to manufacturer's directions for your churn.

Banana-Walnut

Ice Cream

Yield: 3 1/2 quarts

8 eggs separated
2 cups sugar
2 cups whole milk
1 pint heavy whipping cream
2 teaspoons vanilla flavoring
dash of salt
5 bananas, mashed
1 cup chopped walnuts

1. Combine egg yolks with all other ingredients EXCEPT egg whites, bananas and walnuts.
2. Whip egg whites until stiff peaks form.
3. Fold into other mixture.
4. Fold in bananas and walnuts.
5. Pour into the well of an ice cream churn and churn with lots of rock salt and ice according to manufacturer's directions for your churn.

White Chocolate Ice Cream

Yield: 3 quarts

2 cups sugar
1 can sweetened condensed milk
1 large can evaporated milk
4 eggs
1 Tablespoon lemon juice
1 cup white chocolate chips
1 Tablespoon vanilla flavoring
half & half as needed

1. Melt white chocolate chips and evaporated milk in a small saucecpan or double boiler stirring constantly until chocolate is melted.
2. Beat eggs and sugar until frothy.
3. Slowly add white chocolate mixture, stirring constantly.
4. Add remaining ingredients.
5. Pour into the well of an ice cream churn and fill to the "fill line" with half & half.
6. Churn with lots of rock salt and ice according to manufacturer's directions for your churn.

Robin Dudley's
Straw-Ba-Nut Ice Cream

Yield: 1 gallon

6 eggs
2 cups sugar
1 can sweetened condensed milk
1 1/2 teaspoon vanilla flavoring
1 pint fresh strawberries, sliced
2 bananas, mashed
1 cup chopped pecans
8 ounces Cool Whip, thawed
red food coloring
1 cup milk or as needed

1. Beat eggs and sugar.
2. Stir in sweetened condensed milk and vanilla.
3. Mix strawberries, bananas, and pecans.
4. Fold in Cool Whip and add to egg mixture.
5. Add 2 to 3 drops red food coloring to mixture.
6. Pour into well of an ice cream churn and churn with lots of rock salt and ice according to manufacturer's directions for your churn.

Canning and Preserving

Carol's Canned Tomatoes

Mama Kate's Chow Chow

Mother's Scuppernong Jelly

Mother's Pear Relish

Mother's Peach Preserves

Carol's Pickled Okra

Miss Kathleen's Squash Pickle

Squash Relish

Carol's Canned Tomatoes

Yield: your summer crop's overflow

As with most of our older trational southern recipes, there are no exact measurements listed; it was all done by sight and taste. Such is the case with these tomatoes. Miss Carol gave me the pressure cooker times for both pints and quarts. It is entirely up to you and how prolific your garden as to the quanitity you will yield.

ripe red tomatoes
salt
sterilized pint or quart jars
rings and lids for chosen jars

1. Wash, peel and core tomatoes.
2. Coarsley chop and place in a large pot in accordance with the amount of tomatoes on hand.
3. Bring to a boil and cook 10 minutes.
4. Spoon tomatoes into pint or quart jars.
5. Add 1 teaspoon of salt to each pint jar **or** 2 teaspoons of salt to each quart jar.
6. Leave 1/2 inch head space.
7. Adjust lids and rings.
8. Process in pressure cooker:
   Pints-15 minutes at 10 pounds pressure.
   Quarts-20 minutes at 10 pounds pressure.

*Note: To can Tomatoes and Okra, use half tomatoes and half okra and follow the above directions.

Mama Kate's Chow Chow

This is another heirloom Southern recipe. It hails from South Carolina and nearly always graced our Sunday dinner tables. It is perfectly delicious with beans, peas, greens and even hotdogs and hamburgers. The yield varies depending upon the size of the vegetables used. Have plenty of pint jars on hand for this one. This is one of my personal favorites!

1 large or 2 small cabbage
6 green bell peppers
salt
1/2 box dry mustard
2 Tablespoons celery seed
2 Tablespoons tumeric
2 Tablespoons mustard seed
1 teaspoon ground all-spice
1 teaspoon ground cloves
3 pints cider vinegar
6 Tablespoons all-purpose flour

6 large onions
6 hot peppers
4 1/2 cups sugar

1. Remove seeds from hot peppers and bell peppers and shred or grate with all of the vegetables.
2. Sprinkle vegetables evenly with salt to cover.
3. Let stand 1 hour.
4. Combine remaining ingredients in a large saucepan and bring to the boil.
5. Squeeze vegetables to remove excess water.
6. Add to sauce.
7. Return to the boil and cook 30-45 minutes, stirring frequently to prevent sticking.
8. Put in jars and seal.

Mother's Scuppernong Jelly

Yield: 8 half pints

5 cups strained scuppernong juice
7 cups sugar
1 box Sure-Jell

1. Be sure all your jars, lids and rings are clean.
2. Place scuppernong juice in a 6 or 8 quart saucepan.
3. Add Sure-Jell and stir well.
4. Bring quickly to a hard boil, stirring occasionally.
5. Add sugar at once.
6. Cook and stir.
7. When mixture returns to a full rolling boil, cook and stir 1 minute.
8. Remove from heat and skim off foam.
9. Pour immediately into jars.
10. Place lid on jar and screw on ring; invert.
11. Repeat with all jars.
12. Once jars are sealed, stand upright and cool.
13. Store in a cool place.

Mother's Pear Relish

This is perhaps one of my most cherished recipes for mother made this each summer as religiously as she made her Pear Preserves. Only in recent years have I come to appreciate the melange of flavors contained in this age old recipe. Mother referred to one her old secretary's association cookbooks in creating her own version. When I look at her notes in faded pencil in the margins, I truly feel as I did when I was young and she was making this relish. Mother never did write down how many pints it makes. The note simply reads: makes____pints.

1 peck pears	6 large onions
6 green bell peppers	6 red bell peppers
1 bunch celery	3 cups sugar
1 Tablespoon salt	1 Tablespoon all-spice
	(or mustard seed)
5 cups vinegar	

1. Peel and core pears.
2. Run pears, peppers and celery through a food chopper.
3. Add other ingredients and let stand overnight.
4. Put into clean sterile jars with lids and rings.
5. Process 20 minutes at simmering in a hot water bath.

Carol's Pickled Okra

Yield: your garden's overflow

garlic, 1 clove for each jar
hot pepper, 1 for each jar
dill seed, 1 teaspoon for each jar
small okra *(must be small, fresh and tender)*
mustard seed, 1/2 teaspoon per jar *(optional)*

Bring to a boil:
1/2 cup salt
1 quart vinegar
1 cup water

1. Place the peeled garlic and hot pepper in the bottom of a clean, warm, pint jar.
2. Pack the jar firmly with small okra pods.
3. Add dill seed and optional mustard seed to top of each jar.
4. Pour hot brine mixture over okra and spices.
5. Adjust lids.
6. Place in boiling water bath 10 minutes.
7. Let set at least 6 weeks before eating.

Mother's Peach Preserves

Yield: 10-12 pints

1 peck fresh peaches
5 pounds sugar
1 teaspoon salt
12 pint jars with rings and seals

1. Wash peaches; peel and quarter, discarding seed.
2. Place in a large enamel pot or dish pan.
3. Pour sugar over fruit covering well.
4. Cover and let stand overnight.
5. Stir well; begin cooking, <u>uncovered</u>, over medium heat, stirring often.
6. After sugar is melted and fruit begins to boil, reduce heat to medium low.
7. Stir often to prevent sticking.
8. Continue stirring often and cooking for several hours until syrup reaches a desired consistency.
9. Pour into hot sterilized jars and seal.
10. Store when cooled completely.

<u>*Definition:*</u>

Peck-8 quarts

Miss Kathleen's

Squash Pickle

Yield: your garden's overflow

8 cups thinly sliced squash
3 medium bell peppers *(red and green)*, sliced
2 cups sliced onion
1/2 cup salt
2 cups sugar
2 cups vinegar
2 teaspoons celery seed
2 teaspoons mustard seed
1/2 teaspoon ground mustard

1. Combine squash, bell peppers and onions.
2. Cover with cold water and add salt.
3. Soak for 1 hour and drain well.
4. Combine remaining ingredients and bring to the boil and add vegetables.
5. Boil 5 minutes.
6. Pack into sterilized jars and seal.

Squash Relish

Yield: quite a few pints

6 large yellow squash
2 green bell peppers
2 hot peppers
4 onions
1/4 cup salt

1. Grind in food processor.
2. Sprinkle with salt and let stand 1 hour.
3. Drain well.

2 1/2 cups sugar
2 teaspoons tumeric
2 cups vinegar
2 teaspoons celery seed

1. Bring to the boil.
2. Add vegetables.
3. Return to the boil and simmer 10 minutes.
4. Put in sterilized pint jars and seal.

Father's Day Picnic

Homemade Lemonade

Fried Chicken
(Bill's Basics p.215)

Mother's Potato Salad

Nana's Slaw

Fresh Season Fruit

Nana's Deviled Eggs Supreme

Angel Biscuits
(Bill's Basics p.206)

Geneva's Banana Pudding

Homemade Lemonade

Yield: 1 gallon

4 fresh lemons, cut in half
1 1/2 cups hot water
1 1/2 cups sugar
1/2 cup lemon juice

1. Dissolve sugar in hot water.
2. Pour over lemons.
3. Stir well.
4. Shake jug several times.
5. Fill with cold water.
6. Squeeze lemon halves with hands.
7. Replace in jar, discarding lemon rinds.
8. Refrigerate until ready to serve.
9. Adjust tartness with additional lemon juice if desired.

Mother's Potato Salad

Yield: 6 servings

4 or 5 white potatoes, peeled and cubed
3 eggs
mayonnaise *(use own judgement)*
2 to 3 Tablespoons prepared table mustard
3/4 cup sweet pickle relish *(or to taste)*
1/2 cup finely chopped sweet onion
salt and pepper to taste

1. Boil potatoes and eggs in salted water until potatoes are tender 10-12 minutes.
2. Drain potatoes and rinse with cool water and drain again.
3. Peel and finely chop the eggs.
4. Mix with remaining ingredients until desired consistency and flavor is reached.

Nana's Slaw

Yield: 8-10 servings

1/2 of a medium cabagge, finely shredded
2 Tablespoons onion, minced
1 cup baby carrots, shredded
1 stalk of celery, minced
1 cucumber, peeled, seeded and minced
1 Tablespoon cider vinegar
1 Tablespoon sugar
Dukes mayonnaise to moisten
salt and fresh ground black pepper to taste

1. Mix all ingredients well.
2. Adjust seasonings to taste.
3. Cover and refrigerate overnight.

Nana's Deviled Eggs Supreme

Yield: 6 servings

6 eggs
1 teaspoon salt
1 Tablespoon prepared table mustard
2 Tablespoons mayonnaise
1 Tablespoon pickle relish
1 Tablespoon minced green olive with pimento
salt and pepper to taste

1. Place eggs in a small boiler and cover with cold water.
2. Add salt and bring to the boil.
3. Boil 7 minutes.
4. Turn off heat, cover and let rest 5 minutes.
5. Pour hot water off eggs and run eggs under cold water several minutes.
6. Peel eggs and slice lengthwise.
7. Remove yolk portions and combine in a small bowl with remaining ingredients.
8. Season to taste with salt and pepper.
9. Spoon back into egg white halves, cover and chill.

Geneva's Banana Pudding

Yield: 8

3/4 cup sugar   pinch of salt
3 Tablespoons flour   4 eggs
2 cups milk
1/2 teaspoon vanilla flavoring
1 1/2 boxes vanilla wafers
5 medium, fully ripe bananas

1. Mix 1/2 cup sugar, flour and salt in top of a double boiler.
2. Separate eggs; set aside.
3. Heat water in bottom of double boiler.
4. Layer vanilla wafers and bananas in an 8 x 8 inch baking dish; set aside.
5. Beat egg yolks with a fork and add to dry mixture.
6. Gradually add milk, cooking over medium heat.
7. Stir constantly until it thickens as desired.
8. Remove from heat and add vanilla.
9. Pour over layered cookies and bananas.
10. Beat egg white until the soft peak stage.
11. Gradually add remaining sugar and beat until stiff peaks form.
12. Spread evenly over top of pudding, sealing to sides of dish.
13. Bake 5 minutes at 375° until top is lightly browned.

July Fourth in Carolina

Seven Layer Salad

Great Pee Dee Pretzel Salad

Deep Fried Turkey

Baked Beans

Fresh Corn on the Cob

Fresh Cantaloupe and Watermelon

Sliced Tomatoes

Homemade Pickles

Seven Layer Salad

Yield: 8-10 servings

1 head iceberg lettuce, torn into small pieces
1 cup frozen early green peas
1 bunch fresh scallions, chopped
1 green bell pepper, seeded and chopped
1 cup mayonnaise
3 Tablespoons sugar
3/4 cup shredded cheddar cheese
6 slices bacon, cooked and crumbled

1. Layer in a 9 1/2 x 13 inch pyrex casserole the following in order given:

   half the torn iceberg lettuce
   frozen early peas
   scallions
   bell pepper
   remaining half of lettuce

2. Combine mayonnaise and sugar and spread over top lettuce layer.
3. Sprinkle cheese over mayonnaise layer.
4. Sprinkle crumbled bacon over all.
5. Cover and refrigerate overnight before serving.

Great Pee Dee Pretzel Salad

Yield: 10 to 12 servings

2 cups pretzels, crushed
3/4 cup margarine, melted
3 Tablespoons sugar
1 cup sugar
8 ounces cream cheese
2 cups Cool Whip, thawed
3-10 ounce packages frozen sliced strawberries
6 ounces strawberry Jell-O
2 cups boiling water

1. Combine pretzels, margarine and 3 Tablespoons sugar.
2. Press into the bottom of a 9 1/2 x 13 inch pyrex casserole.
3. Bake at 400° for 8-10 minutes.
4. Cool.
5. Mix together cream cheese, sugar and Cool Whip until smooth and creamy.
6. Spoon over cooled pretzel mixture.
7. Dissolve Jell-O in 2 cups boiling water.
8. Add frozen strawberries and pour over cream cheese layer.
9. Cover and refrigerate overnight.
10. Slice and serve as is or over a lettuce leaf.

Deep Fried Turkey

Yield: 10-12 servings depending on size of turkey

2 ounces of each:
        salt
        black pepper
        crushed red pepper
        garlic powder
        Accent seasoning
        chili powder

1. Mix all spices together and rub well into the turkey.
2. Wrap securely and refrigerate and marinate overnight.
3. When ready to cook, heat oil in an outdoor cooker *(fish frying type)*.
4. Insert an opened coathanger into the cavity of the bird making a secure handle that you feel comfortable with.
5. This handle will serve as a means of lowering and removing the turkey from the hot oil.
6. Deep fry the bird for 4 minutes per pound.
7. Be sure to use heavy gloves and have a fire extinquisher nearby.

Baked Beans

Yield: 10 servings

4 each 15 ounce cans pork and beans
1 cup ketchup
1 cup chopped onion
1/2 cup chopped green bell pepper
3/4 cup brown sugar
2 Tablespoons Worcestershire
1 Tablespoon Liquid Smoke
dash of salt
dash of black pepper
6 strips uncooked bacon

1. Combine all ingredients except bacon.
2. Pour into a deep 3 quart casserole dish.
3. Place strips of bacon over the top.
4. Bake uncovered at 350° for 1 1/2 to 2 hours.

Southern Barbeque

Hugh and J.W.'s Brunwick Stew

Barbeque Chicken

Betty Stanley's BBQ Sauce

June's Classic Potato Salad

Nana's Deviled Eggs Supreme
(Father's Day Picnic p.67)

Spicy Bourbon Glazed Spareribs

Aunt Ailene's Coconut Pie

Hugh and J. W.'s Brunswick Stew

Yield: 5 gallons

10 pound chicken
12 pounds fresh pork roast
5 quarts tomatoes or juice
8 each 15 ounce cans corn *(whole kernel or creamed)*
salt and pepper to taste
1/ 2 cup vinegar
5 pounds onions
1 bottle Texas Pete

1. Boil chicken and pork until done, saving chicken broth.
2. Remove all skin from both meats.
3. Cool, debone and chop in a food processor.
4. Chop onion in food processor and add to chicken and pork.
5. Combine all other ingredients with chicken, pork and onion in a very large deep pot.
6. Cook on medium heat to a light boil.
7. Reduce heat and simmer for 1 hour adding chicken broth as needed for desired thickness.
8. Cool and store in airtight containers in refrigerator.
9. Freezes well.

Note: J.W. was my father and Hugh was his brother. They got together often to make large batches of this recipe which they always divided.

Barbeque Chicken

Yield: 8 servings

8 chicken breasts
1 recipe *Betty Stanley's BBQ Sauce p.77*

1. Prepare grill according to manufacturer's directions.
2. Place breasts on grill and cook 3 to 5 minutes per side before applying sauce.
3. Lower flames if using a gas grill, if using regular coals, just be careful.
4. Begin to baste breasts with the sauce, turning to coat.
5 Allow the breasts to cook several minutes after basting so sauce will penetrate the meat.
6. Grill until well done and desired color and thickness of sauce is reached.

Betty Stanley's
BBQ Sauce

Yield: 1 1/2 to 2 cups

14 ounces ketchup
3 Tablespoons brown sugar
1/2 cup water
2 teaspoons liquid smoke
3 teaspoons Worcestershire
3 teaspoons dry mustard
2 teaspoons celery seed
1/4 teaspoon cayenne pepper
1 teaspoon black pepper
3 Tablespoons melted margarine

1. Mix all ingredients well in a small saucepan.
2. Simmer 5 to 10 minutes over low heat.
3. Pour over desired meat or serve on the side.

June's Classic Potato Salad

Yield: 8-10 servings

6 medium golden potatoes, peeled and cubed
4 large eggs, boiled, peeled and chopped fine
1/2 cup sweet pickle relish *(or more to taste)*
1/4 cup minced green bell pepper
4 ounce jar pimento, drained
1 teaspoon celery seed
1 cup Dukes mayonnaise *(more or less to desired texture)*
1 Tablespoon Sauer's prepared mustard
dash of Worcestershire
dash of Tabasco
salt to taste
coarsely ground fresh black pepper to taste

1. Boil potatoes in salted water to cover for 5 minutes or until toothpick tender.
2. Drain and cool.
3. Add remaining ingredients, mixing well.
4. Adjust seasonings to desired taste, cover and refrigerate.

Spicy Bourbon Glazed Spareribs

Yield: 6 servings

12 pounds spareribs
4 Tablespoons Worcestershire
4 Tablespoons brown sugar
6 Tablespoons bourbon
3/4 cup chopped onion
2 Tablespoons chili sauce
1 1/2 teaspoons cayenne pepper
2 cups ketchup

1. Combine all ingredients except ribs.
2. Simmer 30 minutes over a low heat to allow flavors to mingle.
3. Parboil ribs and let them brown slightly as the water boils out.
4. Drain.
5. Pour sauce mixture over ribs and cover in either a large dutch oven or roasting pan.
6. Simmer on stovetop for several hours until tender or bake in covered roaster in the oven at 325º for 2 to 3 hours.

Aunt Ailene's

Coconut Pie

Yield: 8 slices

1 9-inch deep dish pie shell
2 eggs
1 cup sweet milk
1 teaspoon vanilla flavoring
1 cup sugar
2 Tablespoons flour
3/4 stick of butter, melted
1 cup shredded coconut

1. Prick the bottom of the pie shell with tines of of a fork.
2. Mix sugar and flour.
3. Add remaining ingredients.
4. Mix well and pour into prepared pie shell.
5. Bake at 375° for 40-50 minutes.
6. Watch crust carefully to be sure it doesn't burn.
7. If it begins to darken too much, shield it with an aluminum foil collar.

Fancy Fish Dinner

Pecan-Crusted Catfish Fillets

Lime-Cilantro Mayonnaise

Grits and Greens Stuffed Tomatoes

Jalapeno Corn Muffins

Marinated Slaw with Red Peppers

Lemon Sorbet

Pecan-Crusted
Catfish Fillets

Yield: 6 servings

6 nice size catfish fillets
1/2 cup cornmeal
3 Tablespoons flour
1/3 cup finely chopped pecans
dash of salt
1/2 teaspoon cayenne pepper

1. Fill a large skillet with enough oil to shallow fry the fillets; begin to heat.
2. Combine all dry ingredients in a small bowl.
3. Coat fillets thoroughly with dry mixture.
4. Place fillets in hot oil and fry until golden, turning frequently.
5. When fillets are done, drain on paper towels.

Lime-Cilantro Mayonnaise

Yield: 1 1/2 cups

1 1/2 cups good quality mayonnaise
juice and zest of 2 fresh limes
1/2 cup finely chopped cilantro

1. Mix all ingredients well.
2. Keep covered in refrigerator until ready to use.

Grits and Greens Stuffed Tomatoes

Yield: 8 servings

4 tomatoes, halved horizontally
4 Tablespoons butter
6 Tablespoons onion, chopped
1/2 teaspoon garlic, minced
1 cup leftover grits
1 cup cooked turnip greens, well drained
1 1/4 cup cheddar cheese, grated
1/2 teaspoon Worcestershire
1/2 cup pecan, finely chopped
dash of cayenne pepper
salt and pepper to taste

1. After slicing tomatoes, scoop out part of the fruit.
2. Heat butter in a large skillet.
3. Saute onion 5 minutes until clear and tender.
4. Combine all ingredients in skillet, mixing well.
5. Spoon mixture into scooped out tomato halves.
6. Place tomato halves into a greased pyrex dish.
7. Bake uncovered at 350° for 30-40 minutes until tomatoes are tender and topping is golden.

Jalapeno Corn Muffins

Yield: 12 muffins

2 cups grated cheddar cheese
8 ounces sour cream
2 jalapeno peppers, chopped
2 cups self-rising corn meal
1 can of creamed corn
2 eggs, slightly beaten
1/2 cup oil

1. Mix all ingredients well.
2. Pour into greased muffins tins and bake at 350° for 30-45 minutes or until toothpick inserted comes out clean.

Marinated Slaw with Red Peppers

Yield: 8 servings

1 medium cabbage, grated
1 small onion, finely chopped
1 cup cider vinegar
1 teaspoon ground dry mustard
1 teaspoon celery seed
1/2 cup sugar
1 red bell pepper, cut into thin strips
1/4 cup oil
dash of salt
dash of black pepper

1. Combine cabbage, onion and red bell pepper in a medium size bowl.
2. Heat vinegar in a small saucepan and add sugar; cool.
3. Combine with remaining ingredients and pour over cabbage and onion mixture.
4. Cover and refrigerate overnight to let flavors meld.

Lemon Sorbet

Yield: 8-10 servings

1 cup sugar
4 cups water
1 cup fresh lemon juice
grated zest of 1 lemon

1. Place sugar and 1 cup water in a heavy saucepan.
2. Stir until sugar is completely dissolved.
3. Remove from heat and stir in remaining water, lemon juice, and the lemon zest.
4. Chill thoroughly.
5. Churn with plenty of rock salt and ice according to manufacturer's directions for your churn.
6. Garnish with a sprig of fresh mint.

The

Season

of

Autumn

Thanksgiving Remembered

When fall first arrives with its cool crisp mornings and cider scented breezes, I'm carried away to a Thanksgiving of long ago. Autumn in the country at my sister's house in rural South Carolina was a spectacular show! Her yard was scattered with pecans, hidden beneath layers of curly, dead leaves. Fields of cotton were brilliant white against the dark, rich soil. The woods bordering the horse pasture were ablaze with fall colors of red, brown, golden yellow and varying shades of orange.

The restored 1915 farmhouse that stood sentinel to more well-bred times was the traditional setting for our family Thanksgiving gathering. The dining room was elegant; the sideboard laden with a melange of delicacies: a glistening golden roasted turkey, Mama Kate's dressing, cranberry-apple casserole, oyster pie, Mother's candied sweet potatoes and fresh corn and butter beans from the summer harvest.

Mary's antique dining table was dressed in a crisply starched Battenburg tablecloth, her cherished china, crystal and the family silver. An assortment of delicate little dishes filled with pickles, relishes and toasted pecans dotted the table. Batches of fresh hot yeast rolls were nestled in a cloth-lined basket.

A blessing descended over the feast as we stood quiet and thankful and a silence washed over the table as the partaking of the bountiful meal began. When stomachs were full and forks finally laid to rest, conversation flowed as slowly around the dinner table as an afternoon breeze would caress the front porch.

My niece and I were old enough to carry the dishes and had the job of clearing and washing. I don't remember who washed and who dried during that Thanksgiving, but I do recall we reminisced about childhood summers, past family holidays and family that was no longer with us.

We laughed and remembered a lot that afternoon amid the sink of sudzy water and piles of dishesand a new memory was born.

Menus for Autumn

Labor Day at the Lake

Tally Ho! Wagon Finger Foods

Dinner on the Patio

Autumnal Dinner Party

Tailgate Party

Timely Turkey Tips

Traditional Desserts with a Twist

Labor Day at the Lake

Tinye's Three Citrus Chicken

Barbeque Pork Chops

Betty Stanley's BBQ Sauce
(Southern BBQ p.77)

Grilled Corn on the Cob

Milledge House Pasta Salad

Fresh Fruit in Season

Betty Stanley's Lemon-Buttermilk Sauce

Carol's Banana Split Cake

Milledge Street Peanut Butter Pie

Tinye's Three Citrus Chicken

Yield: 6 servings

1/3 cup orange juice
1/4 cup lemon juice
1/4 cup olive oil
1/4 cup honey
3 Tablespoons lime juice
1/4 cup lemon juice concentrate
3 Tablespoons chopped mint leaves
1 Tablespoon orange zest
1 Tablespoon lemon zest
1/4 teaspoon ground cumin
1/4 teaspoon ground cinnamon
dash of salt and black pepper
1/4 of a red onion, thinly sliced
6 chicken breasts *(not boneless)*

1. Whisk all ingredients together and pour over chicken breasts, reserving some of the marinade for later use.
2. Let refrigerate for several hours, but **not** overnight. The enzymes in the citrus will breakdown the chicken and make it non-edible.
3. Prepare grill according to manufacturer's directions and grill breasts 12-15 minutes depending on size, until done.
4. Baste frequently with marinade.

Barbeque Pork Chops

Yield: 6 servings

12 boneless pork chops
1 recipe Betty Stanley's BBQ Sauce
  (Southern BBQ p.)

1. Prepare grill according to manufacturer's directions.
2. Lightly salt and pepper the pork chops.
3. Place on hot grill and sear on both sided for 3-4 minutes.
4. After searing well, begin to baste with barbeque sauce.
5. Continue to grill and baste, turning frequently to coat chops thoroughly.

Grilled Corn on the Cob

Yield 6 to 8 servings

6 to 8 ears fresh corn, still in shuck
1 cup butter, melted

1. Prepare grill according to manufacturer's directions.
2. Open corn gently and remove silks; pull shuck back up over corn.
3. Place corn on grill rack over low burning coals; sprinkle with water.
4. Lower lid and grill for 7-8 minutes.
5. Turn corn and grill 7-8 more minutes.
6. Remove corn from grill and place in a pyrex casserole.
7. Pour melted butter over corn, shucks and all.
8. Wrap entire dish securely in aluminum foil and cover with several dish towels.
9. Let stand 10-15 minutes to allow butter to soak in thoroughly.
10. To serve, pull back shucks or remove entirely.

Note: It is rather dramatic and "earthy" to serve the corn with the shucks intact, yet pulled back from the corn. It makes a very striking presentation and the aroma is good, too.

Milledge House Pasta Salad

Yield: 8-10 servings

3 cups uncooked spiral, tri-color corkscrew pasta
1 1/2 cups Girard's Italian Dressing
3 Tablespoons freshly chopped parsley
2/3 cup pitted black olives, chopped

1. Cook pasta in salted water until done; drain.
2. Combine pasta with remaining ingredients
   and toss well.
3. Cover and refrigerate overnight.
4. Serrve in a lettuce-lined bowl and garnish
   with additional chopped parsley.

*Note: The Girard's Italian Dressing is the key ingredient in this recipe.
I have tried this with other dressings and without success. Girard's brand
has grated Parmesan cheese in the dressing and that adds the needed
touch.*

Betty Stanley's
Lemon-Buttermilk Sauce

Yield: 1 cup

1/2 cup mayonnaise
1/2 cup buttermilk
lemon juice to taste
1 teaspoon poppyseeds

1. Whisk all ingredients together well.
2. Adjust flavoring of lemon juice to suit your own tastes.
3. Delicious with fresh fruit.

Carol's Banana Split Cake

Yield: 12 servings

2 cups graham cracker crumbs
5 Tablespoons butter, melted
2 cups confectioner's sugar
1 stick of butter
1 teaspoon vanilla flavoring
2 eggs
3 or 4 small ripe bananas
14 ounces crushed pineapple, drained
12 ounces Cool Whip
1/2 cup chopped pecans
6 maraschino cherries, halved

1. Combine graham cracker crumbs and melted butter and press into the bottom of a 9 1/2 x 13 inch pyrex dish.
2. Beat confectioner's sugar, 1 stick of butter and vanilla for 10 minutes until creamy.
3. Add eggs and beat well.
4. Spread over crumb mixture.
5. Slice bananas and layer over cream mixture.
6. Spoon drained pineapple over bananas.
7. Frost entire dessert with Cool Whip.
8. Sprinkle with chopped pecans.
9. Place a cherry half on top of each serving.
10. Refrigerate several hours before serving.

Milledge Street
Peanut Butter Pie

Yield: 8 servings

8 ounces cream cheese, softened
1 cup confectioner's sugar
1 cup creamy peanut butter
8 ounces Cool Whip
1 Keebler Chocolate Graham Pie Crust
chocolate syrup for drizzling
additional Cool Whip for garnishing
1/2 cup peanuts, chopped

1. Cream confectioner's sugar and cream cheese until smooth.
2. Add peanut butter and Cool Whip.
3. Beat until creamy and well incorporated.
4. Spoon mixture into pie crust and freeze or refrigerate until ready to serve.
5. Slice pie into eight equal slices and place on dessert plates.
6. Drizzle each slice with chocolate syrup and a spoon of Cool Whip.
7. Sprinkle each topped pie slice with a few chopped peanuts.

*Note: This pie freezes very well and can be made way in advance of use. It is excellent to keep on hand for unexpected company as well.

Tally Ho! Wagon Finger Foods

Fan's Original Cheese Straws
(Dedication p.3)

Refrigerator Cookies

Cinnamon-Sugar Pecans

Pickled Shrimp

Angel Biscuits
(Bill's Basics p.206)

Country Ham

Brie with Almonds and Apricots

Curried Egg Salad with Pumpernickle

Strawberry Muffins with Smoked Turkey

Chilled Beer and Wine

Refrigerator Cookies

Yield: several dozen

1 stick of butter, softened
1 cup light brown sugar, packed
1 cup chopped pecans
1/4 teaspoon salt
1/2 teaspoon baking soda
1 egg
1 3/4 cups all-purpose flour

1. Cream butter and brown sugar.
2. Add remaining ingredients.
3. Form into a long cylinder and wrap in wax paper and refrigerate.
4. Let stand overnight.
5. Slice thin and place on greased baking sheets.
6. Bake on middle rack of oven at 350° until light brown.
7. Watch closely so they do not overbake!

Cinnamon-Sugar Pecans

Yield: 3 1/2 cups

1 cup sugar
1 Tablespoon butter
1/4 cup water
1 1/2 teaspoons ground cinnamon
3 cups shelled, plump pecan halves

1. Bring sugar, butter, water and cinnamon to the boil.
2. Stir continuously for 2 minutes, no longer.
3. Add pecans and stir well to coat.
4. Cool slightly and spread onto wax paper.
5. When cool completely, separate into pieces.

Pickled Shrimp

Yield: 6-8 servings

1 1/2 pounds medium shrimp, boiled and
     peeled
1 lemon sliced thinly
1 red onion sliced thinly
3 bay leaves
1/3 cup vegetable oil
cider vinegar to cover shrimp

1. Layer shrimp, a few lemon slices and onion sliced in a decorative glass bowl.
2. Repeat layers until all ingredients are used.
3. Tuck bay leaves between shrimp to weight them down.
4. Whisk oil and vinegar together.
5. Pour over shrimp.
6. Cover and refrigerate 24 hours.
7. This can be made in a tupperware container for easier handling at outdoor functions.

Brie with Almonds and Apricots

Yield: 8-10 servings

1 cup sliced almonds
1 can apricot halves, drained
1 cup peach preserves
1/2 to 3/4 cup brown sugar
3 wheels miniature brie

1. Remove brie from wooden shaker boxes.
2. Line boxes thoroughly with plastic wrap.
3. Set cheese and boxes aside.
4. In a small saucepan combine apricot halves, peach preserves and brown sugar.
5. Heat, stirring occasionally until sugar is dissolved and mixture is thick.
6. Stir in almonds.
7. Divide the mixture among the 3 brie boxes.
8. Spread evenly in the bottom of each.
9. Place brie wheels on top of mixture.
10. Wrap securely in plastic wrap and return lids to boxes.
11. Refigerate at least 24 hours or longer.
12. To serve, remove lids, unwrap, invert onto serving tray and remove box and plastic wrap.
13. Serve with bland crackers.

Curried Egg Salad

6 large eggs, boiled and peeled
1/2 cup sweet pickle relish
1 Tablespoon Dijon style mustard
1/4 cup chopped olives
1 teaspoon curry powder *(more or less to taste)*
Dukes mayonnaise to moisten
salt to taste
coarsely ground fresh black pepper to taste

1. Chop eggs and combine with all remaining ingredients.
2. Cover and refigerate overnight.
3. Spread on small pumpernickle bread slices to make party sandwiches.

Strawberry Muffins
with Smoked Turkey

Yield: 100 miniature muffins

3 cups all-purpose flour
1 teaspoon salt
1 teaspoon baking soda
3 teaspoons ground cinnamon
2 teaspoons ground allspice
2 each 10 ounce packages frozen strawberries
2 cups sugar
3 eggs, beaten
1 1/4 cups vegetable oil
1 pound thinly sliced smoked turkey

1. Thaw strawberries and puree in blender and set aside.
2. Sift dry ingredients together in a large bowl.
3. Make a well in the center.
4. Add strawberries to remaining ingredients and pour into well.
5. Stir well to moisten all ingredients.
6. Lightly spray miniature muffin tins with cooking spray.
7. Spoon batter into tins and bake at 350° for 10-16 minutes.
8. Turn out from pans and cool on wire racks.
9. Muffins may be frozen at this point and used at a later date.
10. When ready to serve, thaw and slice crosswise and insert a small amount of smoked turkey.

Dinner on the Patio

Tossed Salad Greens
(Bill's Basics p208)

Milledge Street Blue Cheese Dressing

Tarragon Vinaigrette
(Bill's Baiscs p.208)

Oriental Marinade

Marinated Beef Tenderloin

Shrimp and Wild Rice Casserole

Onion-Roasted Potatoes

Broccoli with Garlic Butter

Yeast Rolls
(Easter Sunday Lunch p.29)

Lemon Cheesecake

Chocolate-Coconut Pie

Milledge Street Blue Cheese Dressing

Yield: 2 cups

1 1/2 cups sour cream
1/2 cup mayonnaise
1/4 cup grated onion
4 ounces crumbled blue cheese
salt and white pepper to taste

1. Combine all ingredients until smooth and thick.
2. Cover and refrigerate until ready to use.

Oriental Marinade

Yield: 3/4 cup

1 to 2 buds fresh garlic
1/4 teaspoon fresh ginger, minced
1/4 cup white wine
2 Tablespoons molasses
3 Tablespoons soy sauce
dash of black pepper

1. Whisk all together and pour over desired meat.

Marinated Beef Tenderloin

Yield: 6-8 servings

1 recipe Oriental Marinade *(p. 107)*
3 1/2 pound beef tenderloin

1. Place tenderloin in marinade and let marinate overnight or longer.
2. Prepare grill according to manufacturer's directions.
3. Grill tenderloin over hot coals, turning and basting with marinade until desired doneness.
4. To serve, slice very thin and serve with your favorite sauce.

Shrimp and Wild Rice Casserole

Yield: 8 servings

1 can cream of mushroom soup
1 medium green bell pepper, chopped
1 medium onion, chopped
2 Tablespoons melted butter
1 Tablespoon lemon juice
1/4 teaspoon black pepper
1 cup sharp cheddar cheese, grated
1 package Uncle Ben's Long Grain and Wild Rice
(cooked according to package directions)
1/2 teaspoon Worcestershire
1/2 teaspoon dry mustard
1 pound shrimp, cooked and peeled

1. Mix all ingredients and pour into a greased pyrex casserole.
2. Bake at 375° for 30 minutes until hot all the way through.

Onion-Roasted Potatoes

Yield: 8 servings

1 envelope Onion Soup Mix
2 pounds golden potatoes, cut into chunks
1/3 cup olive oil

1. Preheat oven to 450°.
2. Coat potatoes with oil and dry soup mix.
3. Bake uncovered, stirring occasionally for 40 minutes or until potatoes are tender.

Broccoli with Garlic Butter

Yield: 8 servings

2 bunches fresh broccoli, cut into florets
1 stick butter, melted
2 cloves fresh garlic, minced
salt and white pepper to taste

1. Melt butter in a saute pan or medium size skillet.
2. Add garlic and cook over high heat for 1 minute.
3. Add broccoli and cook quickly for several minutes until broccoli turns bright green and becomes slightly tender.
4. Season to taste with salt and white pepper.
5. Serve hot.

Lemon Cheesecake

Yield: 8-10 servings

1 cup granola
3 Tablespoons brown sugar, packed
1 Tablespoon lemon zest
1 Tablespoon plus 1 teaspoon butter
3/4 cup lemon yogurt
3/4 cup ricotta cheese
1/2 cup cream cheese, softened
2 teaspoons cornstarch
1 teaspoon vanilla flavoring
3 eggs
1/2 cup sugar

1. Combine granola, brown sugar, and 1 teaspoon of lemon zest in a food processor.
2. Process until fine and add butter and process until mixture comes together.
3. Press into the bottom of a 9-inch springform pan and bake for 10 minutes at 350°.
4. Set aside crust.
5. Puree the remaining ingredients in a food processor.
6. When well incorporated, pour gently over the prepared crust.
7. Place cheesecake on a baking sheet and bake for 30 minutes or until set.
8. Cool on wire rack and then refrigerate for 2 hours until chilled.
9. Remove from sides of pan and slice when ready to serve.

Raspberry Sauce

Yield: 1 1/2 cups

2 each 10 ounce packages frozen raspberries
1 Tablespoon cornstarch
2 Tablespoons fresh lemon juice
2 to 3 Tablespoons sugar

1. Puree raspberries in food processor.
2. Strain to remove seeds.
3. Pour into a saucepan.
4. Combine cornstarch and lemon juice and add to raspberry mixture.
5. Bring to a boil until slightly thickened.
6. Chill before serving.
7. Keep in a jar in the refrigerator.

Chocolate Coconut Pie

Yield: 2 pies

2 deep dish pie shells
dash of salt
7 Tablespoons cocoa
1 stick butter, melted
2 cups flaked coconut
1 cup chopped nuts
1 each 12 ounce can evaporated milk

3 cups sugar
4 eggs
1 teaspoon vanilla

1. Mix all ingredients and pour into the 2 pie shells.
2. Bake at 350° for 45 minutes.

Autumnal Dinner Party

Dried Cranberries with Walnuts
and Mixed Greens

Red Wine Vinaigrette

Creamy Turnip Green and Mushroom
Soup

Pork Loin with Plum Sauce

Oriental Rice
(Special Luncheon for Mother p.35)

Broccoli Puree

Bread Pudding with Whiskey Sauce

Dried Cranberries with Walnuts and Mixed Greens

Yield 6-8 servings

3/4 cup dried cranberries
1/2 cup walnuts
1 head bibb lettuce
1 small bunch of fresh spinach
1 head radiccicho

1. Tear all lettuces into bite size pieces.
2. Toss gently and arrange on salad plates.
3. Sprinkle evenly over each plate of lettuces a few cranberries and walnuts.
4. Drizzle with Red Wine Vinaigrette or your favorite dressing.

Red Wine Vinaigrette

Yield: 3/4 cup

1/2 cup red wine vinegar
1/4 cup olive oil
2 teaspoons sugar
dash of salt
1 teaspoon dijon mustard

1. Whisk all ingredients together or mix in a blender or food proccessor until emulsified.
2. Store in jar in the refrigerator.

Creamy Turnip Green and Mushroom Soup

Yield: 8-10 servings

4 Tablespoons butter, melted
1 large onion, thinly sliced
2 cloves garlic, minced
2 cups cooked turnip greens
1 cup fresh sliced mushrooms
salt and fresh ground black pepper to taste
1 quart half and half
2 cups chicken broth or stock
1/2 teaspoon cayenne pepper
3/4 cup Grueyre cheese, grated

1. Saute onion in melted butter for several minutes until transluscent and tender.
2. Add garlic and mushrooms and cook an additional 4-5 minutes.
3. Combine all remaining ingredients seasoning to taste.
4. Puree in food processor and return to stove.
5. Simmer for 20 minutes.
6. Sprinkle with a little Grueyre cheese before serving.

Pork Loin with Plum Sauce

Yield: 8-10 servings

For the pork:

1 whole boneless pork loin
salt and white pepper to taste
2 cloves garlic, pressed or minced
1/2 teaspoon fresh ginger, grated

For the sauce:

1 medium onion, chopped
2 Tablespoons butter, melted
6 ounces frozen lemonade concentrate
2/3 cup chili sauce
12 ounce jar plum preserves
2 Tablespoons soy sauce
2 teaspoons prepared mustard
2 teaspoons sesame seeds
dash of ground ginger

1. To prepare pork, rub salt, pepper, garlic and ginger into meat.
2. Wrap securely in foil, place in a pyrex dish and bake at 350° for 1 1/2 hours.
3. For sauce, saute onion in butter and add to remaining ingredients.
4. Simmer for 30 minutes over low heat.
5. Slice cooled pork loin very thin and drizzle with some sauce.
6. Cover and rewarm for a few minutes.
7. Serve additional sauce on the side.

Broccoli Puree

Yield: 6 servings

2 heads fresh broccoli, trimmed, cut up and most
  of the stalk discarded
salt and black pepper to taste
1/2 cup heavy whipping cream
dash of nutmeg

1. Bring a pot of salted water to the boil.
2. Add broccoli and cook 4 to 5 minutes.
3. The broccoli should be crisp-tender.
4. Reserve about 1/2 cup of water.
5. Puree broccoli in food processor using a small
   amount of water as needed.
6. When all is pureed, return to stove and add
   remaining ingredients.
7. Warm slowly to prevent scorching.
8. Adjust seasonings and serve.

Bread Pudding with Whiskey Sauce

Yield: 8-10 servings

1/4 loaf day old white bread, cubed
1/2 cup butter, melted
6 eggs
1 quart half and half
1 cup sugar
1 teaspoon vanilla flavoring

For the Sauce:
1/2 cup butter
1 1/2 cups confectioner's sugar
1 egg yolk
1/2 cup good whiskey

1. Toast bread cubes and place in a pyrex baking dish.
2. Drizzle with melted butter.
3. Beat remaining ingredients together and pour over bread.
4. Let stand 5 minutes.
5. Bake at 350° for 45 minutes or until golden brown and firm to the touch.
6. Slice into serving size squares and serve with sauce.
7. To make sauce, heat sugar and butter and stir until butter is absorbed.
8. Remove from heat and add egg yolk.
9. Slowly add whiskey.
10. Mixture will thicken as it cools.

Tailgate Party

Cool Chicken Cordon Bleu Sandwiches

Cold Roast Beef Sandwiches

Milledge House Shrimp Salad on Croissants

Marinated Baby Carrots

Jeanie's Cucumber-Onion Salad

Midori Spiked Honeydew

German Chocolate Brownies

Carol's Chewies

Cool Chicken Cordon Bleu Sandwiches

Yield: 4 sandwiches

4 boneless chicken breasts
salt and white pepper to taste
1/2 cup dijon mustard
1/4 cup mayonnaise
4 slices thinly sliced ham
4 slices thinly sliced swiss cheese
4 slices vertical sliced Vlassic Kosher Dill Pickles
4 hoagie rolls, halved lengthwise

1. Sprinkle chicken with salt and pepper.
2. Grill or saute until done.
3. Combine mustard and mayonnaise.
4. Divide and spread on hoagie rolls.
5. Place a chicken breast on the bottom half of hoagie roll.
6. Top each chicken breast with a slice of ham, cheese and pickle.
7. Place top half of hoagie roll on sandwich.
8. Wrap securely in plastic wrap and refrigerate until ready to serve, no more than 24 hours.

Cold Roast Beef Sandwiches

Yield: 4 sandwiches

1 pound thinly sliced roast beef
1/2 cup dijon mustard
2 Tablespoon prepared horseradish
1/2 cup sour cream
4 slices American cheese
4 slices Provolone cheese
4 thin slices red onion
4 fresh kaiser rolls

1. Cut kaiser rolls in half lengthwise.
2. Combine mustard, horseradish and sour cream and spread over both halves of the rolls.
3. Place a few slices of roast beef on the bottom half of each roll.
4. Top with a slice of American cheese.
5. Place remaining roast beef on top of American cheese slices.
6. Top with a slice of Provolone cheese and slice of the red onion.
7. Place top of roll back on sandwich and wrap securely in plastic wrap, but no longer than 24 hours.

Milledge House Shrimp Salad on Croissants

Yield: 4 sandwiches

1 small onion
3 dill pickle strips
2 Tablespoons dried parsley flakes
3/4 cup mayonnaise *(enough to combine)*
dash of garlic powder
1 pound medium shrimp, boiled and peeled
4 croissants

1. Grate onion and dill pickle.
2. Squeeze out excess moisture.
3. Mix with parsley flakes and garlic powder.
4. Coarsely chop the shrimp and mix in the dressing.
5. Store covered in refrigerator no longer than 48 hours.
6. Assemble sandwiches at your party site.
7. A slice of green leaf lettuce and tomato is all this sandwich needs.

Marinated Baby Carrots

Yield: 8-10 servings

1 pound baby carrots
1 bunch scallions, sliced
1/2 green bell pepper, sliced
1 can tomato soup
1/4 cup vegetable oil
3/4 cup cider vinegar
1 cup sugar
1 teaspoon Worcestershire
dash of salt and black pepper

1. Cook carrots in salted water until tender, drain and set aside.
2. In a tupperware container, arrange carrots, scallions and bell pepper.
3. Combine remaining ingredients in a small saucepan and heat throroughly.
4. Pour over vegetables and let cool slightly.
5. Cover and refrigerate 24 hours before serving.

Jeanie's Cucumber-Onion Salad

Yield: 6-8 servings

1 medium onion
2 medium cucumbers
1 envelope Good Seasons Italian Dressing

1. Slice onion and cucumber very thin.
2. Layer in a deep tupperware container.
3. Mix Good Seasons according to package directions and pour over vegetables.
4. Cover and refrigerate overnight.

Midori Spiked Honeydew

Yield: 1 melon or 4-6 servings

1 ripe honeydew melon
3/4 cup midori *(melon flavored liqueur)*

1. Cut a quarter size hole in the top of the melon.
2. Pour midori inside of melon.
3. Plug the hole with the cut piece of melon.
4. Stand melon upright in a bowl in the refrigerator overnight.
5. Strain off midori and slice or cube melon to serve.

German Chocolate Brownies

Yield: 16 brownies

1 1/8 cups all purpose flour
2/3 teaspoon salt
2/3 cup brown sugar
2/3 cup white sugar
1/3 cup cocoa powder
1/2 cup coconut
1/2 cup semi-sweet chocolate chips ·
1/2 cup chopped pecans
3 eggs
1 teaspoon vanilla
2/3 cup oil

1. Mix all ingredients together until moist and well incorporated.
2. Pour into a greased 9 x 9 inch pan and bake at 350º for 27-32 minutes.
3. Test with a toothpick to insure doneness.
4. Cool and cut into squares.

Carol's Chewies

Yield: 36 cookies

1 stick margarine
1 box light brown sugar
3 eggs
2 teaspoons vanilla flavoring
2 cups plain flour
1 cup coconut
1 cup chopped pecans

1. Cream butter and sugar.
2. Add eggs one at a time, beating well after each addition.
3. Add vanilla and flour.
4. The batter will be stiff.
5. Add coconut and pecans by hand.
6. Pour into a greased 9 1/2 x 13 inch pan.
7. Bake at 350° for 30-45 minutes.
8. Cut immediately and cool in pan.

Turkey Roasting Times

Weight	Oven Temperature	Cooking Time
4-5 pound breast	325°	1 1/2 hours
6 pound breast	325°	2 1/4 hours
7 pound breast	325°	2 3/4 hours
10-12 pound turkey	325°	4 hours

Note: for whole turkeys it is safe to figure on 30 minutes per pound in a slow 325° oven.

Sausage-Pecan Dressing

Yield: 20 servings

1 pound mild bulk sausage
2 cups finely chopped onion
1 cup minced celery
1 stick butter, melted
4 cups cornbread crumbs
4 1/2 cups biscuit bread crumbs
dash of salt
dash of black pepper
dash of thyme
4 eggs, beaten
2 1/2 to 3 cups turkey or chicken broth
1 cup chopped pecans

1. Brown sausage, onion and celery until meat is done and vegetables are tender; set aside.
2. Combine remaining ingredients with sausage mixture, stirring well.
3. Use the broth gradually until a texture like thick soup is reached.
4. Pour into a greased 17 x 11 inch pyrex dish.
5. Bake at 350º for 30-45 minutes or until light brown and set.

Oyster Dressing

Yield: 6 servings

1/2 cup onion, chopped
2 Tablespoons butter
2 cups crumbled cornbread
1 cup bread crumbs
3 eggs, beaten
1 Tablespoon Worcestershire
1 teaspoon poultry seasoning
1/4 teaspoon cayenne pepper
1 2/3 cup turkey or chicken broth
8 ounces fresh oysters, chopped

1. Saute onion in butter and add to remaining ingredients.
2. Use broth sparingly until thick, soupy texture is reached.
3. Bake in a greased casserole dish at 350° for 45 minutes to 1 hour or until golden brown firm to the touch.

Pumpkin Cheesecake

Yield: 12-15 servings

1 cup gingersnap cookie crumbs
1/3 cup brown sugar
4 Tablespoons melted butter
1/3 cup chopped pecans
32 ounces cream cheese
4 cups sugar
5 eggs
18 ounce can pumpkin pie filling
3 Tablespoons pumpkin pie spice

1. Mix crumbs, brown sugar and melted butter.
2. Press into the bottom of a greased 9 inch springform pan.
3. Bake at 475° for 8-10 minutes or until a light golden; set aside.
4. Beat cream cheese and sugar until fluffy.
5. Add eggs, one at a time, beating well after each addition.
6. Add pumpkin pie mix and spice.
7. Beat well.
8. Pour into crust and bake at 325° for 1 hour and 45 minutes.
9. Refrigerate at least 12 hours before serving.
10. Top with a spoon of whipped cream if desired before serving.

Huguenot Torte

Yield: 6 servings

1 egg
3/4 cup sugar
2 Tablespoons flour
1 1/4 teaspoons baking powder
1/8 teaspoon salt
1/2 cup nuts, chopped
3/4 cup fresh apple, peeled and chopped
1 teaspoon vanilla

1. Beat egg until lemon colored and fluffy.
2. Gradually add sugar and beat until smooth.
3. Sift flour, salt and baking powder together.
4. Add to egg and sugar mixture.
5. Add nuts, apple and vanilla.
6. Grease well an 8 x 8 inch pan.
7. Pour in batter and bake at 325° for 45 minutes.
8. Top with whipped cream before serving if desired.

Mama Kate's Apple Cake

2 cups sugar
1 1/2 cups vegetable oil
3 cups plain flour
1 teaspoon baking soda
1 teaspoon baking powder
1 teaspoon ground ginger
1 teaspoon ground cinnamon
1 teaspoon salt
2 teaspoons vanilla flavoring
3 eggs
3 cups chopped apples, unpeeled
1 cup chopped pecans
1 cup chopped date

1. Combine sugar and oil.
2. Add eggs.
3. Combine all dry ingredients in a bowl and mix with sugar/oil mixture.
4. Add apples, nuts, dates and vanilla.
5. Pour into a greased and floured tube pan and bake at 325° for 1 1/2 hours.
6. Cool in pan 10 minutes before turning out.
7. Top with the following glaze:

   1/2 stick butter
   1/4 cup evaporated Pet milk
   1 cup brown sugar

1. Bring to the boil and boil 5 minutes.
2. Pour over warm cake.

The

Season

of

Winter

Menus for Winter

Soups for Supper

New Year's Eve Dinner for Two

A Winter Lunch with a Neighbor

Comfort Foods to Carry

Valentine's Dinner for Two

Soups for Supper

Spicy Chili

Creamy Wild Rice and Mushroom Soup

Bourbon Corn Chowder

Joanne's Sour Cream Muffins

Broccoli Cornbread

Hummingbird Cake

Spicy Chili

Yield: 6-8 servings

2 pounds ground chuck
1 medium onion, chopped
1 can chopped tomatoes
1 Tablsepoon chili powder
1/2 teaspoon cayenne pepper
1 cup chili sauce
1 teaspoon salt
1/2 teaspoon black pepper
1 can tomato sauce
1 cup beer
1 can red kidney beans, drained
1 cup shredded extra sharp cheddar cheese

1. Brown ground chuck and onions until meat is done and onions are clear and tender.
2. Drain off grease.
3. Add remaining ingredients except beer.
4. Adjust seasoning to suit your own taste.
5. Add beer and simmer 30 minutes.
6. Add beans and simmer 10 more minutes.
7. Serve and top with a sprinkling of cheese.

Creamy Wild Rice and Mushroom Soup

Yield: 8 servings

2 boxes Uncle Ben's Long Grain and Wild Rice
  Blend-Original Recipe
1 pound fresh mushrooms, sliced
1/2 cup sherry
1 quart half and half
salt and white pepper to taste

1. Cook rice according to package directions.
2. Add mushrooms 3 minutes before rice is to complete cooking.
3. Add sherry and half and half.
4. Season to taste with salt and white pepper.
5. Let simmer 20 minutes.
6. Mixture will thicken in refrigerator overnight and more liquid will have to be added before reheating and serving.

Bourbon Corn Chowder

Yield: 6 servings

1/2 stick butter, melted
1 onion, chopped fine
2 1/2 cups cream style corn
1/2 cup bourbon
salt to taste
black pepper to taste
1/2 cup chicken stock
1/2 cup half and half
3 slices bacon, cooked and crumbled

1. Melt butter and saute onion until tender.
2. Add remaining ingredients except bacon and simmer for 30 minutes.
3. When ready to serve, sprinkle a little bacon over each serving.

Sour Cream Muffins

Yield: 24 miniature muffins

1 cup sour cream
1 cup self-rising flour
1 stick of margarine, melted

1. Mix all well.
2. Spoon into greased miniature muffin pans.
3. Bake at 400° for 15-20 minutes.

Broccoli Cornbread

Yield: 12 servings

10 ounces frozen chopped broccoli, thawed
1 large onion, chopped
8 ounces cottage cheese
1 stick butter, melted
4 eggs, beaten
1 teaspoon salt
1 package Jiffy corn muffin mix

1. Mix all ingredients well.
2. Bake at 400º for 30 minutes or until golden and firm to the touch.

Hummingbird Cake

Yield: 12 servings

3 cups all-purpose flour
2 cups sugar
1 teaspoon salt
1 teaspoon baking soda
1 teaspoon ground cinnamon
3 eggs, beaten
1 1/2 cups vegetable oil
1 1/2 teaspoons vanilla flavoring
8 ounces crushed pineapple, undrained
2 cups chopped pecans
2 cups chopped bananas

1. Combine dry ingredients and add beaten eggs and oil.
2. Stir until dry ingredients are moistened.
3. DO NOT STIR!
4. Add the vanilla, crushed pineapple, nuts and bananas, stirring only to incorporate.
5. Pour into 2 greased 10 x 10 square dishes.
6. Bake at 350º for about 30 minutes or until a tester comes out clean.

Icing:
1 stick margarine, softened
8 ounces cream cheese, softened
2 teaspsoons vanilla flavoring
1 box confectioner's sugar
1 cup chopped pecans

1. Beat until fluffy and spread on cake.
2. Sprinkle top with nuts.

New Year's Eve Dinner for Two

Ann Parker's Crab Stew

Bitter Winter Salad

Easy Vinaigrette

Bavarian Pork Chops

Sauteed Squash with Dill

Milledge Street Broccoli Casserole

Yeast Rolls
(Easter Sunday Lunch p.29)

Quick Praline Ice Cream

Dianne's Cinnamon Sauce

Ann Parker's Crab Stew

Yield: 6-8 servings

2 cans cream of potato soup
2 cans cream of celery soup
4 soup cans milk
1 medium onion, chopped
3/4 stick margarine
1 pound crabmeat
1 pint half and half
1/4 cup sherry

1. Saute onion in margarine until done.
2. Add all remaining ingredients.
3. Simmer over low heat until hot all the way through.
4. Serve with crackers or croutons.

Bitter Winter Salad

Yield: 6 servings

1/2 pound broccoli raab
1/2 pound kale
6 stalks swiss chard
1 head romaine lettuce
1 cup shaved white cheddar cheese

1. Wash and tear greens and toss.
2. Arrange on individual salad plates.
3. Artfully arrange shavings of cheese over each salad.
4. Drizzle with Easy Vinaigrette or your favorite dressing.

Easy Vinaigrette

Yield: 1 cup

1/2 olive oil
1/2 cup red wine vinegar
dash of salt
1 Tablespoon fresh rosemary leaves

1. Emulsify all ingredients in a blender until well mixed.
2. Drizzle over salad when ready to serve.
3. Store covered in the refrigerator.

Bavarian Pork Chops

Yield: 6 servings

6 center cut pork chops
1/2 cup all purpose flour
1 teaspoon ground thyme
1 teaspoon garlic powder
dash of salt
1 bunch of scallions, chopped, roots trimmed
1/2 pound mushrooms, sliced
1/2 stick of margarine, melted
12 ounces warm beer

1. Combine flour, thyme, garlic powder, and salt in a small bowl.
2. Dredge pork chops, coating well on both sides.
3. Saute scallions and mushroom in melted margarine 2 minutes.
4. Place pork chops on top of vegetables and cover for 3 to 4 minutes.
5. Uncover and turn mixture over, some vegetables will remain on bottom.
6. Cook pork chops 3-4 minutes on this side.
7. Remove to a pyrex casserole and pour all pan drippings over pork chops.
8. Pour warm beer over all and cover casserole with a piece of alumninum foil.
9. Bake at 350º for 30-45 minutes until done.

Sauteed Squash with Dill

Yield: 6 servings

6-8 small or medium squash, ends trimmed
1 clove of fresh garlic, minced
1 Tablespoon fresh dillweed
3 Tablespoons olive oil
salt and white pepper to taste

1. Slice squash into relatively thin slices.
2. Heat olive oil in a small skillet.
3. Add squash and saute for 3 to 5 minutes until they begin to go slightly limp.
4. Add garlic and dillweed and cook for a few more minutes.
5. Season to taste with salt and pepper.

Milledge Street Broccoli Casserole

Yield: 8 servings

2 each 10 ounce packages chopped broccoli
1 medium onion, chopped
1 cup cooked white rice
1 cup shredded cheddar cheese
1 can cream of mushroom soup
1 teaspoon Worcestershire
1/2 cup mayonnaise
salt and black pepper to taste

1. Cook broccoli and onion in salted water until broccoli is tender; drain well.
2. Combine with remaining ingredients.
3. Pour into a greased pyrex casserole dish and bake at 350° for 20-30 minutes or until hot all the way through.

Quick Praline Ice Cream

Yield: 8-10 servings

1 cup butter, melted
1/2 cup brown sugar
2 cups all-purpose flour
1/2 cup oatmeal
1 cup chopped pecans
1 jar caramel ice cream topping
1/2 gallon vanilla ice cream, partially softened

1. Combine first 5 ingredients in a pyrex casserole dish and bake at 350° for 30 minutes, stirring several times.
2. Cool mixture and gently fold into softened ice cream.
3. Swirl in caramel topping.
4. Pour into a rectangle tupperware container with a lid and freeze.
5. Spoon out into individual serving dishes and serve with your favorite sauce.

Dianne's Cinnamon Sauce

Yield: 1 cup

1 /4 cup sugar
1 Tablespoon cornstarch
1 cup water
3 Tablespoons lemon juice
1 Tablespoon butter
1 teaspoon cinnamon
1/2 teaspoon numeg

1. Combine sugar and cornstarch.
2. Mix all ingredients in a small saucepan.
3. Simmer over low heat, stirring until mixture boils and thickens.

A Winter Lunch with a Neighbor

Raspberry Congealed Salad

Chicken and Asparagus Casserole

Broiled Herbed Tomatoes

Parmesan-Herb Biscuits

Assorted Pickles

Chocolate-Coconut Pie
(Dinner on the Patio p.113)

Raspberry Congealed Salad

Yield: 8 servings

6 ounces raspberry Jell-O
1 1/2 cups boiling water
1 pack frozen raspberries, thawed *(or strawberries)*
1 cup applesauce
1 cup chopped pecans

1. Dissolve Jell-O in boiling water.
2. Combine with remaining ingredients.
3. Pour into a pyrex casserole dish and chill until firm.
4. Cut into squares and top with the following:

> 1/2 cup mayonnaise
> 1/2 cup sour cream

1. Whisk together.
2. Spoon on salad square.

*Note: This is a beautiful burgandy salad and is particularly striking when served on a bed of red leaf lettuce. The colors really set one another off and are very eye appealing.

Chicken and Asparagus Casserole

Yield: 8 servings

4 boneless chickend breasts, boiled and cubed
2 cups cooked white rice
1 can cream of chicken soup
1 cup mayonnaise
1 teaspoon curry powder
1 teaspoon lemon juice
2 cans asparagus tips, drained
1 cup grated cheddar cheese

1. Arrange rice in the bottom of a 9 1/2 x 13 inch casserole dish.
2. Arrange chicken on top of rice.
3. Arrange asparagus on top of chicken.
4. Mix soup, mayonnaise, curry and lemon lemon juice and spread over all.
5. Work a spoon down into the casserole to help distribute the sauce.
6. Sprinkle cheese over all and bake until hot all the way through.

Broiled Herbed Tomatoes

Yield: 6 servings

3 ripe red tomatoes
2 Tablespoons olive oil
1 Tablespoon fresh garlic, minced
1 Tablespoon fresh basil, minced
1 Tablespoon fresh parsley, minced

1. Slice tomatoes in half crosswise.
2. Brush each cut half with olive oil.
3. Sprinkle each half with garlic and herbs.
4. Place on a baking sheet and run under broiler until bubbly and edges begin to char.

Parmesan-Herb Biscuits

Yield: 3 dozen

2 cups self rising flour
1/4 cup plus 1 Tablespoon shortening
2/3 cup buttermilk
3 Tablespoons grated Parmesan cheese
1 teaspoon parsley flakes
1 teaspoon dillweed
1 teaspoon basil

1. Combine flour and shortening.
2. Stir in buttermilk, cheese and herbs.
3. Roll out with a 1 1/2 inch round cutter.
4. Bake at 450° until golden brown.
5. Brush tops with melted butter.

Comfort Foods to Carry

Carolina Baked Vegetables

Milledge House Squash Casserole

Chocolate-Coconut Pie
(Dinner on the Patio p.113)

Original Breakfast Casserole

Candy Bar Pie

Creamy Leek and Potato Soup

Chicken and Asparagus Quiche

Carolina Baked Vegetables

Yield: 6 servings

2 large yellow squash, sliced
4 large tomatoes, sliced
2 large zucchini, sliced
3 medium onions, sliced
salt and pepper taste
1 1/2 sticks margarine
Parmesan cheese, grated
1 cup mozzarella cheese, grated

1. Layer vegetables in a pyrex casserole.
2. Dot each layer with butter and sprinkle each layer with Parmesan cheese, salt and pepper.
3. Tomatoes should be last layer, do not dot this layer or sprinkle with cheese.
4. Bake uncovered at 350º for 45 minutes to 1 hour.
5. Top with mozzarella cheese and return to oven until cheese melts and begins to brown.

Milledge House Squash Casserole

Yield: 6-8 servings

1 pound yellow squash, sliced
1 large onion, sliced
1 cup cheddar cheese, grated
1/4 cup butter
2 eggs
1/2 cup mayonnaise
10 saltines, crushed
1 teaspoon Worcestershire
salt and pepper to taste

1. Slice squash and onion and cook in boiling water until tender; drain.
2. Combine with remaining ingredients and pour into a buttered casserole dish.
3. Bake at 350° for 30 minutes.
4. Top with crushed saltines and bake an additional 5 minutes.

Original Breakfast Casserole

Yield: 8 servings

6 slices white bread
butter
1 pound sausage, cooked, drained and crumbled
2 cups chedded cheese, grated
5 eggs
2 cups half and half
1 teaspoon dry mustard
1/2 teaspoon pepper

1. Butter both sided of white bread and cut into cubes.
2. Place cubes in a buttered pyrex casserole dish.
3. Sprinkle with sausage and cheese.
4. Whisk eggs, half and half and spices together.
5. Pour over mixture in casserole.
6. Cover and chill overnight.
7. Remove from refrigerator 20 minutes before baking.
8. Bake at 350° for 40 to 50 minutes.

Candy Bar Pie

Yield: 8 servings

1/2 gallon vanilla ice cream, softened
8 ounces Cool Whip
1 Butterfinger candy bar
1 Snickers candy bar
1 Reeses Cup
1 Hershey Bar
1 Crunch candy bar
1 chocolate graham cracker pie shell
chocolate syrup
additional Cool Whip
maraschino cherries

1. Beat ice cream in a mixer until creamy.
2. Add Cool Whip.
3. Crush all candy bars and add.
4. Pour into the pie shell.
5. Freeze.
6. To serve, drizzle with chocolate syrup, put on a dollop of Cool Whip and top with a cherry.

Creamy Leek and Potato Soup

Yield: 9 cups

3 small potatoes, washed and peeled
2 leeks, washed, trimmed, and sliced
2 Tablespoons butter
6 cups milk
1 1/2 teaspoons salt
1/4 teaspoon black pepper
1 teaspoon chicken boullion granules
1 to 1 1/2 teaspoons dried oregano
1 1/2 cups instant potatoes

1. Cook potatoes in boiling water to cover for 15 minutes or until tender, drain.
2. Saute leek in butter in a large pot.
3. Stir in next 5 ingredients.
4. Cook over low heat stirring constantly until hot.
5. Remove from heat and stir in potato flakes and potatoes.
6. Serve sprinkled with crumbled bacon and parsley flakes.

Chicken and Asparagus Quiche

Yield: 8 servings

1/2 cup Bisquick
2 large eggs
2 cups whole milk
1 teaspoon dry mustard
1 cup cooked chicken, cubed
1/2 cheddar cheese, grated
1 can asparagus tips, drained

1. Layer chicken, cheese and asparagus in an 8 x 8 inch casserole dish.
2. Combine Bisquick, milk, eggs and dry dry mustard in a blender.
3. Blend on high 1 minute.
4. Pour batter over filling mixture.
5. Bake at 350º for 45 minutes or until puffy and golden.

Valentine's Dinner for Two

Crab and Red Pepper Bisque

Mixed Greens with Pears, Walnut and
Roquefort

Tarragon Vinaigrette
(Bill's Baiscis p.208)

Bacon Wrapped Beef Filet

Mixed Grilled Vegetables

Crab-Stuffed Potatoes

White Chocolate Almond Ice Cream

Coffee Praline Sauce

Crab and Red Pepper Bisque

Yield: 8 servings

4 medium red bell peppers, chopped
2 leeks, chopped *(white portion only)*
1 medium onion, chopped
3 Tablespoons butter, divided
2 cups chicken broth
2 cups whipping cream
1 cup white crabmeat
salt and white pepper to taste

1. In a large saucepan saute peppers, leeks and onions in 1 Tablespoon butter.
2. Add broth and cream.
3. Increase heat and simmer until reduced by 1/3, about 30 minutes.
4. Puree in blender until smooth.
5. Return mixture to saucepan and add crabmeat.
6. Simmer 15 minutes.
7. Add salt, white pepper and remaining butter.
8. Serve hot.

Mixed Greens with Pears, Walnuts and Roquefort

Yield: 6 servings

1 cup romaine lettuce, torn
1 cup red leaf lettuce, torn
1 cup butter lettuce, torn
1 cup green leaf lettuce, torn
2 pears, cored and sliced
1 cup walnuts pieces, toasted
1/2 cup Roquefort cheese, crumbled

1. Toss all salad greens.
2. Arrange on salad plates.
3. Arrange pear slices on each salad.
4. Sprinkle walnuts and cheese over each salad.

Bacon Wrapped Beef Filet

Yield: 4 servings

4 beef tenderloin filets
4 slices bacon
8 shallots
1/2 cup brandy
8 sprigs fresh thyme

1. Wrap a piece of bacon around each filet.
2. Secure with a toothpick.
3. Gently insert a few sprigs of thyme between bacon and filet.
4. Place in a shallow, foil-lined baking pan and place 2 shallots on top of each filet.
5. Drizzle brandy over all.
6. Carefully, using a match, ignite the brandy and allow it to burn itself out.
7. Cover the filets with additional foil and bake at 375º for 25 minutes or until desired doneness.

Mixed Grilled Vegetables

1 yellow squash, sliced
1 zucchini, sliced
1 red bell pepper, sliced
1 green bell pepper, sliced
1 onion, cut into 8 wedges
1 cup cherry tomatoes
1 clove fresh garlic, pressed
1 Tablespoon fresh parsley, chopped
1 Tablespoon fresh thyme, chopped
1/2 cup olive oil
2 Tablespoons balsamic vinegar

1. Wrap grill rack in foil.
2. Pierce foil several times for ventilation.
3. Prepare grill according to manufacturer's directions.
4. Combine olive oil, garlic, herbs and vinegar.
5. Place all vegetables on the foil wraped rack.
6. Toss around frequently to insure even even cooking.
7. Periodically drizzle vegetables with olive oil mixture.
8. Grill 10-12 minutes until vegetables appear slightly tender and begin to char around edges.

Crab Stuffed Potatoes

Yield: 6 servings

6 baking potatoes
2 Tablespoons butter, softened
1 cup sour cream
1 small onion, grated
1 teaspoon salt
1/4 teaspoon cayenne pepper
8 ounces crabmeat
paprika
1/2 cup grated swiss or cheddar cheese
3 scallions, finely chopped

1. Bake potatoes at 400° for 1 hour.
2. Poke with fork after 30 minutes to allow steam to escape.
3. While warm, cut in half lengthwise and scoop out inside.
4. Mash potato, butter, sour cream, onion and seasonings until smooth.
5. Stir in crabmeat.
6. Lay the potato skins on a baking sheet and fill.
7. Sprinkle with paprika and bake for 15 to 20 minutes at 375°.
8. Remove from oven and sprinkle with cheese.
9. Run under broiler to melt cheese.
10. Sprinkle with scallions before serving.

White Chocolate-Almond Ice Cream

Yield: 3 quarts

2 cups sugar
1 can sweetened condensed milk
1 large can evaporated milk
4 eggs
1 Tablespoon lemon juice
1 cup white chocolate chips
1 Tablespoon almond extract
1 cup sliced almonds
half & half as needed

1. Melt white chocolate chips and evaporated milk in a small saucepan or double boiler stirring constantly until chocolate is melted.
2. Beat eggs and sugar until frothy.
3. Slowly add white chocolate mixture, stirring constantly.
4. Add remaining ingredients.
5. Pour into the well of an ice cream churn and fill to the "fill line" with half & half.
6. Churn with lots of rock salt and ice according to manufacturer's directions for your churn.

Coffee Praline Sauce

Yield: 3 cups

1 1/2 cups light brown sugar
2/3 cup light corn syrup
4 Tablespoons butter
5 ounce evaporated milk
1 teaspoon vanilla
2/3 cup chopped pecans
1 Tablespoon instant coffee

1. Combine sugar, syrup and butter.
2. Heat to boiling.
3. When cooled to lukewarm, add milk and blend well.
4. Stir in vanilla, pecans and coffee.
5. Store in refrigerator

Christmas:

A

Season

of

its

Own

Christmas Eve

Christmastime has always been special to me and as I've grown so has my understanding and appreciation of the holiday season. Yuletide memories flood my mind and fill me with such excitement that I plan for Christmas all year long.

As a caterer I am usually busy until the last minute, even delivering orders Christmas Eve morning. Late in the afternoon I begin the long drive my sister's home in South Carolina. The drive is peaceful and my spirit unwinds to the soothings chords of Handel's Messiah and other seasonal music. I arrive shortly after dark; the house an elegant beacon. Windows glow warmly with cheerfully winking candles and soft luminious lamplight. A plume of smoke curls up from the woodburning stove in the den, its woodsy smell penetrating the cold, bitter night.

I enter to melodious hum of of cheerful voices and the rich aroma of a savory repast. Mary, my sister, always serves a hearty arrayof hors'doeuvres, eggnog and wine.

Later we take communion at a rustic Pine Grove Church, each of us lost in our own quiet remembrances. We return to the warmth and charm of William and Mary's and her melange of delicacies.

Conversation lulls on through seemingly endless hours of eating and drinking, remembering and laughing. As the temperature drops and the hour wanes, we clear dishes and put away remaining savories. Christmas Eve culminates with an eleven o'clock carol servie. The majesty and glory of Christmas unfolds as soloist, duet and choir bring into focus the holiness of the season.

At midnight all voices unite in the singing of Silent Night and the church bells ring, celebrating Christ's birth.

Christmas has arrived surrounded by family and friends, uplifted with song and filled joy and goodwill toward men. I hope these recipes and reminiscences will evoke a feeling of peace on earth for you, your family and your friends as you prepare to celebrate the season of Christmas.

Menus for Christmas

Chrismas Eve Cocktails

Christmas Breakfast

Christmas Day Dinner

Christmas Cookies

Christmas Eve Cocktails

Christmas Punch
Grand Marnier Eggnog
Angel Biscuits
(Bill's Basics p.206)
Sliced Turkey
Cranberry-Orange Relish
Shrimp Dip
Milledge Street Sand Dollars
Cocktail Meatballs
Curried Chutney Cheese
Hot Chicken and Sausage Dip
Hot Mexican Dip
Crab Stuffed Mushrooms
Ham Wrapped Asparagus
Dill Pickle and Ham Sandwiches
Sesame Thins

Christmas Punch

Yield: 1 gallon

1 quart eggnog
1/2 large bottle club soda
1/2 gallon vanilla ice cream, softened

1. Stir all together.
2. Pour into punch bowl
3. Sprinkle top with crushed peppermint candies.
4. Decorate punch bowl with candy canes.

Grand Marnier Eggnog

Yield: 12 servings

6 eggs, separated
2 cups sugar
1/4 cup bourbon
1 cup Grand Marnier *(orange flavored liqueur)*
2 cups heavy cream
2 cups milk
grated nutmeg for garnish
4 Tablespoons sugar

1. Beat the egg yolks well in a bowl and set aside.
2. Add sugar and beat well.
3. Stir in heavy cream and milk.
4. Stir in bourbon and Grand Marnier.
5. Pour into punch bowl.
6. Beat egg whites until stiff peaks form and add remaining sugar and spoon over eggnog.
7. Sprinkle lightly with nutmeg.

Cranberry Orange Relish

Yield: 2 cups

1 pound fresh cranberries
1 whole seedless orange
1 1/2 cups sugar

1. Coarsely chop cranberries and orange in a food processor.
2. Add sugar and put in a jar in the refrigerator at least 24 hours before serving.
3. Excellent with turkey or ham and makes a nice accompaniment on little sandwiches.

Shrimp Dip

Yield: 12 to 15 servings

1 pound cream cheese, softened
1 cup sour cream
1 onion, minced
2 pounds shrimp, peeled, cooked and chopped
7 ounce can of shrimp, drained and mashed.

1. Mix all together.
2. Spread in a small glass dish.
3. Serve with crackers.

Milledge Street Sand Dollars

Yield: 8 dozen

2 sticks margarine
1/2 cup sugar
1 teaspoon vanilla flavoring
1/2 cup crushed potato chips
1/2 cup chopped pecans
2 cups all purpose flour
confectioner's sugar for dusting

1. Cream margarine, sugar and vanilla.
2. Add potato chips and pecans.
3. Add flour.
4. Chill dough 1 hour.
5. Roll into walnut sized balls.
6. Flatten with a glass dipped in granulated sugar.
7. Bake at 350° for 16-18 minutes or until light brown.
8. When cool, lightly dust with powdered sugar.

Cocktail Meatballs

Yield: 50 meatballs

2 pounds ground beef
salt and black pepper
46 ounces ketchup
10 ounces pepper jelly

1. Form beef into walnut size balls.
2. Layer in a pyrex dish.
3. Sprinkle with salt and black pepper.
4. Cover with foil and bake at 350° for 1 hour.
5. Melt pepper jelly in a large saucepan.
6. Add ketchup, stirring well.
7. When meatballs are done, drain well and add to sauce.

Curried Chutney Cheese

Yield: 1 ball

24 ounces cream cheese
3/4 cup chutney, pureed
curry powder to taste
1/2 cup chopped pecans

1. Combine all and form into a ball.
2. Garnish top with pecan halves.
3. Serve with crackers.

Hot Chicken and Sausage Dip

Yield: 3 cups

16 ounces cream cheese, softened
3 scallions, chopped fine
1 pound sausage, browned and crumbled
1 cup chicken, cooked and cubed
1 cup sour cream
1 Tablespoon Worcestershire

1. Mix all ingredients well.
2. Cover and bake at 325° 30 minutes or until hot all the way through.
3. Serve in a chafing dish with crackers.

Hot Mexican Dip

Yield: 8-10 servings

8 ounces cream cheese, softened
10 ounces Bunker Hill Chili without beans
8 ounces Jalepeno Cheese

1. Spread cream cheese in the bottom of a 9 1/2 x 13 inch pyrex.
2. Top with chili.
3. Slice jalepeno cheese and layer over chili.
4. Bake at 375° until bubbly.

Crab Stuffed Mushrooms

Yield: 20 servings

40 large mushrooms
1/2 cup Parmesan cheese
1/2 cup bread crumbs
1/4 cup grated onion
2 cloves garlic, minced
dash of salt
dash of pepper
1 cup white crabmeat
1 stick butter, melted
3 ounces cream cheese

1. Remove stems from mushrooms and chop fine.
2. Combine remaining ingredients and mix well.
3. Spoon into mushroom caps.
4. Place on a baking sheet and bake at 350° for 10-15 minutes.
5. Serve hot.

Ham Wrapped Asparagus

Yield: 10 servings

2 pounds fresh asparagus, ends trimmed
1 bottle Girard's Italian Dressing
1 pound thinly sliced ham

1. Blanch asparagus in hot water 1 to 2 minutes.
2. Rinse under cold water to stop cooking process.
3. Place in a tupperware container and cover with dressing.
4. Marinate overnight.
5. Drain asparagus and wrap each spear with a slice of ham.
6. Arrange wagon wheel fashion on a round serving platter.

Dill Pickle and Ham Sandwiches

Yield: 12 servings

6 slices white bread, crusts removed
4 ounces cream cheese, softened
3 Tablespoons mayonnaise
6 slices ham
6 baby dill pickles

1. Flatten bread slices.
2. Mix cream cheese and mayonnaise.
3. Spread a thin layer of cream cheese mixture over each bread slice.
4. Place a thin ham slice over each cheese layer.
5. Place a dill pickle at one end of the sandwich and roll up jelly roll fashion.
6. Squeeze gently.
7. Rolls can be refrigerated and sliced later.
8. When ready to serve, slice each roll into 6 slices.
9. This sandwich has a nice pinwheel effect.

Sesame Thins

Yield: about 3-4 dozen

2 cups sifted all purpose flour
1/2 teaspoon baking soda
1/2 teaspoon salt
1 cup butter
1 cup sugar
1 egg
1 teaspoon vanilla
1/2 cup sesame seeds

1. Sift flour, soda and salt into a small bow.
2. Cream butter with sugar until fluffy.
3. Add egg and vanilla.
4. Stir in flour mixture a little at a time.
5. Wrap mixture in plastic wrap and chill several hours or until firm enough to handle.
6. Roll dough into small balls and then in sesame seeds.
7. Bake at 350° for 10-12 minutes.

Christmas Breakfast

Sausage and Mushroom Quiche

Dianne's Creamy Grits
(Garden Club Brunch p.20)

Strawberry Bread
(Tally Ho! Wagon Finger Foods p.105)

Angel Biscuits
(Bill's Basics p.206)

Mother's Pear Preserves
(Dedication p.4)

Mother's Peach Preserves
(Canning and Preserving p.60)

Sausage and Mushroom Quiche

Yield: 8 servings

1/2 cup Bisquick
2 large eggs
2 cups whole milk
1 teaspoon dry mustard
1 pound sausage, cooked and crumbled
1 cup sliced fresh mushrooms
1/2 cup cheddar cheese, grated

1. Layer sausage, mushrooms and cheese in an 8 x 8 inch casserole dish.
2. Combine Bisquick, milk, eggs and dry mustard in a blender.
3. Blend on high 1 minute
4. Pour batter over filling.
5. Bake at 350° for 45 minutes or until puffy and golden.

Christmas Day Dinner

Cranberry Congealed Salad

Roast Turkey with Herbs

Mother's Cornbread Dressing
with Giblet Gravy
(Bill's Basics p.210)

Turnip Greens
(Bill's Basics p.216)

Oyster Pie

Candied Sweet Potatoes
with Grand Marnier and Pecans

Cranberry-Orange Relish
(Christmas Eve Cocktails p.176)

Yeast Rolls
(Easter Sunday Lunch p.29)

Japanese Fruitcake

Ambrosia

Cranberry Congealed Salad

Yield: 12-15 servings

2 cups fresh cranberries
2 cups sugar
6 ounces cherry Jell-O
1/2 cup lemon juice
2 cups hot water
1 cup cold water
2 envelopes Knox unflavored gelatin
1 cup celery, chopped
1 cup chopped pecans
1 whole orange, ground in food processor
1 cup crushed pineapple

1. Grind cranberries and add to orange.
2. Add sugar and stir well.
3. Let this mixture stand at least 1 hour.
4. Dissolve Jello-O in hot water, gelatin in cold water.
5. Combine Jell-O and gelatin, add lemon juice, celery, nuts and crushed pineapple.
6. Stir well and add to cranberry mixture.
7. Pour into a casserole dish or decorative mold and refrigerate until firm.

Roast Turkey with Herbs

Yield: 10-12 servings

1 whole turkey, giblet bag removed and saved
1 grannysmith apple, quartered
1 orange, quartered
1 onion, quartered
1 bunch fresh parsley
1 bunch fresh thyme
1 bunch fresh rosemary
salt

1. Rinse turkey well inside and out; pat dry.
2. Sprinkle inside cavity lightly with salt.
3. Place fruit, onion, and herbs inside of bird.
4. Secure turkey's legs together and place on roasting tray in roasting pan.
5. Cover and bake at 325° for 30 minutes per pound or until a thermometer registers 170°.
6. Cool and remove stuffing ingredients.
7. Slice turkey and arrange on a serving platter.
8. Garnish with sprigs of fresh herbs.

Oyster Pie

Yield: 8 servings

1 pint of fresh oysters
1 box Nabisco oyster crackers, crushed
1 stick margarine
salt and pepper to taste
2 cups milk *(or more if needed)*

1. Drain oysters.
2. Put a layer of oysters in a greased casserole.
3. Sprinkle with salt and pepper.
4. Cover with cracker crumbs and dot with butter.
5. Repeat using all ingredients; top layer should be cracker crumbs.
6. Cover with milk and bake at 350° for about 30 minutes. Do not allow to boil.

Candied Sweet Potatoes with Grand Marnier and Pecans

Yield: 6-8 servings

1 cup sugar
3/4 cup water
1/4 teaspoon salt
1/2 cup butter
2 large, red sweet potatoes, peeled
1/2 cup white corn syrup
3 Tablespoons Grand Marnier
1/2 cup chopped pecans

1. Slice sweet potatoes into strips.
2. Mix water, sugar, salt, butter and syrup in a large, heavy skillet.
3. Heat to boiling.
4. Drop the strips into the boiling mixture.
5. Reduce heat and cook uncovered, slowly for 1 to 1 1/2 hours.
6. Shake pan frequently to prevent sticking, but do not stir. It will break up potatoes.
7. When ready to serve drizzle with Grand Marnier and sprinkle with pecans.

Japanese Fruitcake

Yield: 16 servings

3 cup all purpose flour
1 1/2 cups sugar
1 cup butter
3 teaspoons baking powder
1 teaspoon salt
1 cup buttermilk
1 cup golden raisins
2 cup chopped pecans
1 Tablespoon ground allspice
1 Tablespoon ground cinnamon
1 Tablespoon ground cloves
4 egg yolks
4 egg whites, beaten

1. Cream butter and sugar.
2. Add egg yolks, mixing well.
3. Mix baking powder, salt and spices with flour.
4. Add alternately with buttermilk to egg mixture.
5. Dredge raisins and pecans in flour to prevent them from sinking during baking.
6. Fold raisins and pecans into batter.
7. Fold in beaten egg whites.
8. Pour batter into 3 greased baking pans and bake at 350° until cakes tests done.
9. Ice with Japanese Fruitcake Icing.

Japanese Fruitcake Icing

grated rind and juice of 2 lemons
3 cups sugar
2 cups hot water
2 Tablespoons flour
3 egg yolks
2 cups grated coconut

1. Mix all ingredients except coconut and cook until it begins to thicken.
2. Add coconut.
3. Spread on cake layers while still warm.

Ambrosia

Yield: about 1 gallon

3 dozen seedless oranges
14 ounces crushed pineapple
24 ounces Topic Isle grated coconut
1 1/2 cups sugar *(sweeten to taste)*

1. Cut oranges in half and remove pulp.
2. Squeeze excess juice from oranges.
3. Place orange meat and juice in a gallon jar.
4. Add pineapple, coconut and half the sugar.
5. Stir well and taste.
6. Add more sugar as needed.
7. Cover and store in refrigerator until ready to use.

Christmas Cookies

Jeanie's Ginger Crinkles

Ruth's Stove Top Cookies

Jeanie's Sugar Cookies

Ruth's Sugar Cookies

Tinye's Almond Biscotti

Ruth

I was obviously destined to become a caterer-my life was surrounded and influenced by food. At nearly every stage in my life food played a significant part. There were many people who helped shape my culinary career. One such person was daddy's niece, Ruth.

Cousin Ruth lived in Germany while her husband, George, was in the army. When they returned to Georgia, they moved into a house several streets away from us. It was more than a house. It was a world full of unusual, interesting and beautiful objects. Her yard was unimaginable. It was a horticulturist's heaven of roses, daisies, sweet peas, hydrangeas, day lilies, peaches, figs, nectarines, plumns, pears, scuppernongs, squash, tomatoes, cucumbers and hot peppers. Ruth was very talented. She did crochet and needlepoint, made exquisite ornaments of felt, sequins and beads. She make jellies, preserves and pickles and cooked everything from German delicacies to plain old southern victuals. How I admired dear Ruth with her unique charm, her style and her flare for "doing". Simply put, she was a motivator. She loved Christmas best of all and her house at that time is forever in my memory.

Ruth always put her tree up Thanksgiving Day. It was decorated with unusual wooden and glass ornaments from Germany and her own handmade creations. It kept me enthralled for hours. Her walls were decorated with wooden

German cuckoo clocks, which chimed ceremoniously throughout the day.

Ruth always increased her flurry of bread, cookie and candy making during the holidays, making great quantities of each for sharing. Her cookies were artistic jewels decorated with lemon flavored icing and garnished with edible dragees and sprinkles.

I was entranced by Ruth's creativity and clever energy. and set goals to be like her. She could accomplish more in one day than anyone else I knew. She was always busy on some project or creation. I was devestated when she died suddenly one October afternoon. The shock reverberated throughout our entire family. That night I sat alone save the company of her rose bushes, and I cried.

That happened well over 15 years ago. I still think of her everyday. I am motivated by my memories of her and am inspired by her ornaments that still adorn our tree. I inherited her cookware, sturdy and German-made, and I use it whenever I cater. Each Christmas when I roll out a batch of her sugar cookies or hang the wooden cuckoo clock ornament on the tree, I think of dear Ruth: the motivator, the cook, the gardner, my mentor, my cousin and friend.

Jeanie's Ginger Crinkles

Yield: about 3-4 dozen

2/3 cup oil
1 cup sugar
1 egg
4 Tablespoons molasses
2 cups flour
1 teaspoon baking soda
1 teaspoon baking powder
1/2 teaspoon salt
1 teaspoon cinnamon
2 teaspoons ground ginger

1. Mix oil with sugar.
2. Add egg and beat well.
3. Stir in molasses.
4. Sift dry ingredients together and add.
5. Drop by teaspoonfuls into 1/4 cup sugar.
6. Drop onto greased cookie sheet.
7. Bake at 350° for 10 minutes.

Ruth's Stove Top Cookies

Yield: 4 dozen cookies

2 cups sugar
1 stick butter
1/2 cup milk
2 Tablespoons peanut butter
2 Tablespoons cocoa powder
1 teaspoon vanilla
3 cups quick cooking oats
1 cup chopped pecans

1. Place sugar, butter, milk and peanut butter in a saucepan.
2. Heat to boiling and stir until sugar is dissolved.
3. Remove from heat and add cocoa, vanilla, oats and nuts.
4. Stir well and quickly.
5. Drop by teaspoonfuls onto waxed paper.
6. Cool and store in airtight tins.

Jeanie's Sugar Cookies

Yield: 3 dozen

2/3 cup butter
3/4 cup sugar
1 egg
1/2 teaspoon vanilla
2 cups all purpose flour
1/4 teaspoon salt
4 Tablespoons milk

1. Cream butter and sugar; add egg.
2. Add vanilla, flour, salt and milk.
3. Roll out on floured board and cut into desired shapes and sprinkle with colored sugar.
4. Place on greased baking sheet and bake at 375° for 10-12 minutes.

Ruth's Sugar Cookies

Yield: 4-5 dozen

1/2 cup butter
1/2 cup shortening
1 cup sugar
3 eggs
3 1/2 cups sifted all purpose flour
1 teaspoon baking soda
2 teaspoons cream of tartar
1 1/2 teaspoons vanilla flavoring

1. Cream butter, shortening and sugar.
2. Add eggs, blending well.
3. Sift flour, soda and tartar.
4. Add gradually to creamed mixture.
5. Add vanilla.
6. Chill do until firm enough to handle.
7. Roll out on floured board and cut into desired shapes.
8. Bake at 375° for 8-10 minutes.

Tinye's Almond Biscotti

Yield: 3 dozen

1 3/4 cups plain flour
1/2 teaspoon baking soda
1/2 teaspoon baking powder
1/8 teaspoon salt
1/2 cup unsalted butter, at room temperature
2 Tablespoons grated orange zest
1 1/2 teaspoons vanilla flavoring
2 eggs
1 1/2 cups shelled almonds, coarsely chopped

1. Sift together flour, soda, powder and salt in a bowl; set aside.
2. Combine butter, sugar, orange zest and vanilla in a large bowl; beat until fluffy.
3. Add eggs, one at a time, beating well after each addition.
4. Add almonds.
5. Add flour mixture until just incorporated.
6. Cover and chill for at least 1 hour.
7. Preheat oven to 350º and butter a large cookie sheet.
8. Divivde dough in half and shape each into a log 1 1/2 inches in diameter.
9. Place on baking sheet and bake about 30 minutes or until light brown and firm.
10. Cool slightly and and slice each on the diagonal into 3/4 inch slices.
11. Place cut side down on baking sheet and bake 15 minutes; cool.

Bill's

Basics:

A Guide for Beginners

Making Stocks

Stocks are rich liquids made from bones and vegetables and have been universally known as the basis for soups, stews, and sauces in nearly every culinary genre for ages. Pasta and grains can also be cooked in stocks. Stocks are slow simmered to insure thy have rich color and robust flavor. True hearty stocks will require an entire morning or afternoon for preparation, but the final result will be well worth the time and effort. Preparing stocks takes us the very root of culinary arts. Today with lack of time or skill the preparation of stocks from scratch has become almost obsolete except in select home kitchens and prefessional "gourmet" restaurants.

The idea that making stocks is difficult is a major misconception. There is really nothing to fear. Most stocks are begun with bones and cuts of inexpensive meat. Though cuts of meat are excellent for this because they are virtually useless for anything other cooking. I prefer to roast the bones and meat in a hot oven until they are well browned. This gives richer flavor and deeper color; however, bones may be placed directly in the stockpot without browning. Occasionally coating the bones with tomato paste while roasting will increase the over all color and flavor. A layer of mire poix (vegetables and pronounced meer pwa), is added on top of the bone layer. Mire poix generally consists of roughly cut or chopped celery ribs, carrots and onions. It is not necessary to fine cut them; slicing the celery and carrots into 3 or 4 pieces and quartering the onion is sufficient. I toss in a few bay leaves. Traditionally bay leaves are inside the "bogquet garni", but I like to see them floating in the stock. Following the addition of vegetables, fill

*the stockpot with cold water to cover the ingredients. Toss in
the bouquet garni of herbs and spices and turn up the heat.
Bring the stock to the boil and and immediately reduce the heat
and maintain at a simmer. Add hot water as the water level
drops and skim the foam from the surface. 3 or 4 hours later,
or longer, strain the stock through a cheesecloth-lined sieve and
cool thoroughly before storing.*

*Each stock type such as beef, veal, chicken, fish and
vegetable has a specified formula. For best results, follow the
directions carefully. The following guidelines and definitions
should, I hope, make preparing stock less forboding.*

Terminology

<u>Bouquet Garni</u>~an assortment of herbs and
spices usually bound in a cheesecloth pouch.
These aromatics are simmered with the stock and
removed when strained. They usually consist of
bay leaves, black peppercorns, cloves and stick
cinnamon.

<u>Marrow</u>~the center tissue of a bone. Marrow
provided robust flavor and a natural gelatin that
allows stocks to "congeal" when cooled.

<u>Mire poix</u>~vegetables cut and used for roasting
with meat and bones: usually carrots, celery and
onions.

Guidelines for Stock Making

♦ Always begin stocks in cold water.
♦ For a darker stock, roast meat and vegetables in a hot oven. For reddish brown stock with richer, hearier flavor, paint the bones with tomato paste pior to roasting.
♦ Select cuts of meat and bone that have a minimal amount of fat, but enough meat and marrow to impart a robust flavor.
♦ Keep the foam skimmed from the surface of simmering stock. Bitter impurities float to the top and if left in will create a cloudy, bitter stock.
♦ When ready to strain the stock, ladle it, do not pour and this will keep any impurities from mixing in with the good stock.
♦ For stocks with bones as their primary substance, better results will be obtained with a longer simmering time of 6-8 hours.
♦ For best use, freeze the stock in convenient amounts in plastic containers, freezer bags or ice cube trays.
♦ Do not add salt to stock until the very end because of reduction.

Angel Biscuits

Yield: 6-7 dozen small biscuits

6 cups self rising flour
1/4 cup sugar
1 cup shortening plus 2 Tablespoons
1/4 teaspoon salt
1/4 teaspoon baking powder
1 teaspoon baking soda
2 ounces dry yeast
1/4 cup lukewarm water
2 cups buttermilk

1. Sift flour, sugar, salt, baking powder and soda together.
2. Cut in the shortening using a fork or pastry blender.
3. Dissolve yeast in 1/4 cup warm water.
4. Add yeast and buttermilk.
5. Knead well.
6. Roll out on floured board or counter.
7. Cut into rounds and place on greased baking sheets.
8. Bake at 425° for 10 to 12 minutes.
9. Brush tops with melted butter.

Basic Vanilla Ice Cream

Yield: 1 gallon

2 cups sugar
1 can sweetened condensed milk
1 large can evaporated milk, chilled
3 pints sweet milk
4 eggs
1 Tablespoon lemon juice
1 Tablespoon vanilla flavoring

1. Beat eggs and sugar together until creamy.
2. Add remaining ingredients.
3. Pour into churn and fill to "fill line" with whole milk.
4. Churn with lots of ice and rock salt according to manufacturer's directions for your churn.

Tossed Salad Greens

Yield: 8 cups

2 cups iceburg lettuce, torn
2 cups red leaf lettuce, torn
1 cup radicchio, torn
2 cups romaine, torn
1 cup fresh spinach, torn

1. Mix torn greens well in a large bowl.
2. This is a very colorful mixture with varied flavors.

Tarragon Vinaigrette

Yield: 1 cup

1/2 cup tarragon vinegar
1 Tablespoon dijon mustard
3 Tablespoons confectioner's sugar
1/2 cup vegetable oil
1 Tablespoon chopped tarragon

1. Combine all ingredients in a blender until thick and emulsified.
2. Store in jar in the refrigerator.

Mother's Cornbread Dressing with Giblet Gravy

Dressing yield: 12-14 servings

9 inch cake biscuit bread
9 inch cake cornbread
1 cup celery, chopped fine
1/2 cup onion, chopped fine
6 eggs, separated
1 1/2 quarts turkey or chicken broth

1. Crumble bread into a large bowl.
2. Pour warm broth over bread and let stand 15 minutes to soften.
3. Mash with potato masher until consistency of thick soup.
4. Cook celery and onion in a small amount of water for about 10 minutes.
5. Pour into broth mixture.
6. Beat egg yolks and add to mixture.
7. Beat egg whites until stiff and fold into mixture.
8. Pour into a large greased casserole and bake at 350º for 30-45 minutes until light brown.
9. Do not overbake. Dressing sets up and dries out as it cools.
10. Dressing will hold, covered, in the refrigerator for several days.

Giblet Gravy

Yield: about 2 cups

1 chicken liver
1 chicken gizzard
2 Tablespoons flour
2 whole eggs
1 cup milk
1/2 cup cold water

1. Cook liver, gizzard and eggs in 1 cup water until all are done.
2. Lift out liver, gizzard and eggs.
3. Peel eggs and chop.
4. Chop gizzard and liver.
5. Add to cooking water.
6. Salt and pepper to taste.
7. Make a thickening of 1/2 cup cold water and 2 Tablespoons flour.
8. Add milk to cooking water and meat.
9. Add thickening and stir well.
10. Bring to the boil and reduce heat.
11. Stir until desired consistency is reached.
12. May be made ahead and reheated.

Lemon-Mustard BBQ Sauce

Yield: 2 cups

2 lemons, sliced
2 Tablespoon butter
1/2 cup chopped onion
1/2 cup brown sugar
1 Tablespoon liquid smoke
dash of Worcestershire
1/2 cup Sauer's prepared mustard
1/4 cup water
1/4 cup cider vinegar

1. Place all ingredients in a medium saucepan.
2. Bring to the boil and reduce heat.
3. Simmer 20-30 minutes.
4. Baste on desired meat and grill.

Wine Poached Chicken

Breasts

Yield: 8 breasts

8 bone in chicken breasts
3 cups water
1 cup white wine
1/2 onion, sliced
cheese cloth bundle of:
>   1 Tablespoon whole allspsice berries
>   1 teaspoon whole black peppercorns
>   1 piece stick cinnamon
>   2 bay leaves

1. Place chicken breasts in a large pot with cold water and wine.
2. Layer onion sliced on top.
3. Tie up cheesecloth bundle of herbs and place in pot under water level.
4. Bring to the boil and reduce heat to low and maintain at a simmer for 1 to 1/2 hours.
5. Liquid may be strained and used for other cooking.
6. These cooked breasts are suitable for use in salads, stews or casseroles.

Julie Dwyer's Tea Syrup

Yield: 1 gallon

12 family size tea bags
12 cups water
6 1/2 cups sugar

1. Bring water to the boil.
2. Remove water from heat, insert tea bags and cover.
3. Let stand for 10 minutes.
4. Remove tea bags.
5. Add sugar while tea is still warm.
6. Stir until dissolved.
7. Store in covered jug in the refrigerator.
8. Will keep a week or more.
9. When ready to mix, use 1 cup syrup to 4 cups water.

Ice Rings and Molds

ring mold of your choice
pineapple juice to fill mold
fresh strawberries
fresh grapes
lemon wedges
lime wedges

1. Fill ring mold to nearly full and place in freezer.
2. When partially frozen, arrange fruit decoratively on top of juice so that it will be frozen to the juice.
3. Use toothpicks to secure if necessary.
4. Place entire mold in freezer and freeze until set.
5. Wrap in plastic wrap until ready to use.
6. To unmold, heat bottom in hot water for a few seconds.
7. Place mold in punch bowl.
8. As it reaches room temperature, you will see the fruit take on a frosty appearance.

Fried Chicken

Yield: 6-8 servings

2 pound fryer chicken
1 cup Crisco oil
salt to taste
black pepper to taste
flour for dredging

1. Cut chicken in desired pieces, or have butcher cut it for you.
2. Salt and pepper as desired.
3. Pour Crisco oil into a large frying pan.
    (adjust amount of oil to size of pan.)
4. Heat oil over medium heat until hot enough to begin frying.
5. Dredge chicken with flour.
6. Add half of chicken to hot pan.
7. Cook 10-15 minutes or until lightly browned and golden on bottom.
8. Turn chicken to other side and cook an additional 10-15 minutes until lightly browned and golden.
9. Continue cooking and turning until pricked pieces run clear juices.
10. Remove from grease and drain on paper towels.

Turnip Greens

Yield: 6-8 servings

2 bunches fresh turnip greens, with roots
3 slices of bacon or 3 Tablespoons drippings

1. Remove roots and stems.
2. Wash greens thoroughly, 3 or 4 times.
3. In a large pot with a small amount of water place greens and boil until leaves are completely wilted.
4. In a smaller pot bring to boil the bacon slices in approximately 1 cup water.
5. Add wilted greens, salt to taste.
6. Cook covered on low heat for 1 hour.
7. Peel and slice the roots and add to the pot of greens.
8. Cook for at least 1 hour longer.
9. Stir often.
10. Add one teaspoon sugar if desired.
11. Keep covered in refrigerator or freeze.

Tartlet Shell Dough

Yield: 24 small shells

1/4 cup butter plus 3 Tablespoons, softened
3 ounces cream cheese, softened
1 cup all purpose flour

1. Cream butter and cream cheese.
2. Add flour, mixing well.
3. Roll into 24 small balls and press into the bottom and up sides of miniature muffin tins.
4. Bake at 400° until lightly browned.
5. Cool on wire racks.
6. Shells may be frozen at this point or filled with filling of your choice and served.

Pie Dough Hints

- Have all ingredients at room temperature.
- Excess fat will produce greasy, crumbly dough.
- Chill pie dough to tenderize and keep it from shrinking during baking.
- All dough to rest 1 hour at room temperature before rolling or handling.
- Be sure to cut pie crusts 2 inches larger than selected pan. Pastry wheels with crinkled or fluted edges make fun decorative edges.
- If pies require a long baking time, place them on baking sheets to keep their bottoms from burning.
- Freeze unfilled tart shells in tupperware containers with sheets of waxed paper between them. Thaw on wire racks and fill accordingly.
- For unbaked crusts when a filling is used, do not prick the bottom of the shell, but lightly brush the crust with egg white to keep it from getting too soggy.

Plantation Tea Punch

Yield: 20 servings

1 small lemonade concentrate
1 small orange juice concentrate
2 cups pineapple juice
1/2 gallon strong tea, unsweetened
2 cups sugar to taste

1. Mix all ingredients in a large bowl or jar.
2. When ready to serve, pour into punch bowl filled with crushed ice.
3. Garnish with fresh lemon slices and mint sprigs.

Chicken Stock

Yield: 6 cups

1 chicken
3 carrots, peeled
1 onion, peeled and quartered
2 red onions, peeled and quartered
3 celery stalks, cut in 1 in pieces
1 bunch fresh parsley
4 bay leaves
1 teaspoon whole black peppercorns
1 teaspoon whole cloves
cheesecloth
twine

1. Place parsley, bay leaves, peppercorns and cloves on a square of cheesecloth and tie up.
2. Place chicken and vegetables in a large pot and cover with water.
3. Add bouquet garni.
4. Bring up to the boil and reduce heat.
5. Simmer for 3 to 4 hours, watching the water level and skimming foam from surface.
6. Strain and cool.
7. Refrigerate, freeze or use.

Beef Stock

Yield: 3 cups

3 pounds beef shank bones, cut into pieces
4 beef short ribs
2 large onions, quartered
4 carrots, chopped
4 stalks of celery cut in pieces
3 fresh bay leaves
2 sprigs fresh thyme
2 sprigs fresh parsley
1 Tablespoon black peppercorns
cheesecloth
twine

1. Place herbs and peppercorns on a square of cheesecloth and tie up.
2. Place bones, meat and vegetables in a roasting pan and roast uncovered at 375° for 20-30 minutes until well brown.
3. Remove to a large pot and cover with water.
4. Add bouquet garni and bring to the boil.
5. Reduce heat and simmer for 3 to 4 hours.
6. Strain and cool.
7. Store in refrigerator, freeze or use.

Herb and Spice Glossary

Keep in mind this listing is only partial and focuses on the more popular, widely used and more readily available herbs and spices found in general cooking. As one continues to cook, one will accumulate a wider variety of seasonings. Growing a small herb garden can be rewarding, fun and cost effective. I enjoy my large pots of mixed herbs and use them frequently.

Allspice~a pungent dried berry or seed pod with a flavor of cinnamon, nutmeg and cloves, thus its name. It is found whole or ground; used in sweet potatoes, various pies, cakes and some marinades.

Basil~a spicy, almost hot, flavored herb. Fresh is better; used in soups, sauces, stews and Italian and Mediterranean recipes.

Bay Leaf~a woodsy herb, somewhat pungent, is usually sold dry. It is used in soups, stews, marinades and sauces.

Cayenne~a finely ground red chili pepper. Extremely hot and should be used in moderation. It is used in a variety of ways from sauces to meat dishes.

Chervil~a very delicate basil flavored herb. It has a short shelf life. Delicious in cheese, egg, and poultry recipes.

Chives~an onion-like herb with a mild flavor. Either fresh or dried are available. For use in a variety of dishes to impart a mild, subtle onion flavor.

Cilantro~also called Chinese parsley. It has a very distinctive flavor. Fresh is best. It is used in salsas and in dry rubs and marinades.

Cinnamon~a sweet-hot spice that is actually the bark of a tropical tree. Found in sticks or ground. Used mostly in baking and some pickling.

Clove~named for its nail-like shape. It is extremely pungent and sweet. It is found whole or ground. Used in sweet and savory recipes.

Curry Powder~actually a blend of up to twenty spices. Used primarily in Indian recipes.

Dill~a delicate, feathery herb. Best fresh; dried will do. A medium pungent flavor. Used in salads, soups and stews.

Mint~a strong brilliant green herb. Best fresh; used in teas, desserts and lamb recipes.

Mustard Seed~spicy pungent spice is found dried both yellow and brown varities. Used for making mustards, marinades and in some pickling.

Nutmeg~a nutty, very pungent spice used mostly in baking. Usually found ground. Use lightly.

Oregano~A member of the mint family. Primarily used in Italian recipes. Very pungent. Fresh or dried varities are available.

Paprika~ground dried red peppers. Usually on the sweet side. Used in stews and as a garnish when sprinkled on food.

Parsley~not very strong in flavor, but makes up for it in eye appeal. Comes in 2 varities-curly or flat leaf. Used fresh for garnishing or dried for seasoning and sprinkling.

Rosemary~a fragrant piney herb. Either fresh or dried is usable. Used mostly in stews, meat and fish recipes.

Sage~a fuzzy herb. Strong flavored. Fresh is better but dried, rubbed sage works well, too. Used in pork, poultry and casserole recipes.

Tarragon~a licorice flavored herb. Mainly used in chicken and shellfish recipes. Either fresh or dried works well. Tarragon vinegar is also good when used in salad dressings.

Tumeric~nearly flavorless it is used mainly for its yellow color. Used in some pickling recipes. It is usually found in its ground form.

General Glossary

Aspic~a jelly made from the cooking liquids of beef or poultry; often strengthened with additional gelatin and is used for coating and garnishing cold foods.

Bake~to cook cakes, pies, cookies, breads and similar pastries as well as meats, fish and casseroles in an oven by dry heat.

Baste~to ladle pan fat, marinade or other liquid over food as it roasts in order to add flavor, to tenderize and to prevent drying out while cooking.

Blanch~to plunge foods quickly into rapid boiling water for a brief period, then into cold ice water.

Blend~to mix two or more ingredients together until smooth and incorporated.

Boil~to cook food in a liquid at a high temperature where bubbles are formed in the liquid and break the surface.

Bouillon~a clear stock made from poultry, beef or veal, plus vegetables, seasonings and liquid.

Braise~to brown in fat and cook covered in a small amount of liquid.

Bread~to coat with bread or cracker crumbs, usually after dipping in egg or milk.

Broil~to cook under a direct heat source.

Chop~to cut into small pieces.

Cream~to beat two ingredients together until smooth, light and fluffy, as in butter and sugar when making cake batter.

Crimp~to pinch or press the edges of a dough together with fingers, fork, or decorative tool, to form a sealed edge or to seal in a filling.

Cube~to cut into large or medium uniform squares.

Dash~a very small amount, less than 1/16 of a teaspoon.

Deep Fry~to cook food covered in hot, temperature controlled fat.

Deglaze~to loosen the browned bits in a skillet or roasting pan with a liquid while stirring and heating.

Dice~to cut into small uniform cubes.

Dot~to scatter bits of butter or seasonings over the surface of a food to be cooked.

Drain~to pour off excess liquid.

Dredge~to coat with flour or crumbs prior to frying or cooking.

Drizzle~to pour melted fat or liquid over a food in a thin stream.

Dust~to cover lightly with flour, confectioner's sugar, cocoa powder or other dry ingredient.

Fold~to incorporate ingredients in a gentle over and under motion.

Garnish~to decorate a food item colorfully and creatively to make it more appealing.

Glaze~to coat a food with a syrup or other liquid so that it glistens when cooked.

Grease~to coat a pan or casserole with a small amount of fat to prevent foods from sticking when cooked.

Grill~to cook over direct heat on a grill usually with charcoal or a similar element of heat.

Grind~to pulverize into a fine coarse in a food mill or food processor.

Julienne~to cut into uniform slivers or slender strips.

Knead~to work a dough gently with the hands until it is smooth and springy.

Macerate~to allow foods to steep in alcohol or other liquids.

Marinade~the liquid in which food is allowed to steep to tenderize it and impart more flavor.

Marinate~to steep foods in a seasoned liquid.

Melt~to heat a solid until it becomes liquid.

Meringue~a stiff mixture of sugar beaten with raw egg whites, then traditionally baked.

Mince~to cut into fine pieces.

Mix~to stir together to incorporate ingredients.

Poach~to cook in barely simmering liquid such foods as fish or poultry.

Puree~to pulverize foods until a smooth, velvety texture is reached.

Reduce~to boil a liquid until the quantity is decreased.

Roast~to cook meat or poultry in the oven by high indirect dry heat.

Roux~a cooked fat-flour mixture used to thicken sauces and gravies.

Saute~to cook quickly in a small amount of fat at a high heat.

Score~to make shallow criss-cross cuts of the surface of a food with a sharp knife.

Sift~to put flour or another dry ingredient through a fine sieve or sifter to aerate.

Simmer~to cook in a liquid at or much below the boiling point.

Skim~to remove fat or film from the surface of a liquid or sauce.

Soak~to let food stand in a liquid.

Steam~to cook covered on a trivet or in a specially made device over a small amount of boiling water.

Steep~to all food to soak in a liquid until the liquid absorbs the flavor.

Stew~to cook, covered in a simmering liquid.

Stir~to mix with a spoon, spatula or fork using a circular motion.

Stock~a liquid flavor base of soups and sauces made by slow cooking of meats, fish or poultry with their bones.

Whip~to beat vigorously until frothy.

Zest~the oily, aromatic rind of citrus fruits.

Common Measures

When I am calculating the amound needed for a catering event or perhaps a dinner party I am having in my own home, I like to plan on serving 3 portions from a cup of vegetables, rice and salads. If serving heavy soup such as a bisque or gumbo a 6 to 8 ounce serving is adequate. A lighter soup can be generously served in 8 to 10 ounce portions. When calculating your meat proportions, plan on 4 to 6 ounces of meat per person is it is a boneless meat; 6 to 8 ounces of meat if there is bone in the meat. It is far more hospitable to err on the side of generosity and have leftovers, than to miscalculate and run out. A piece of meat will look large and more than adequate at the market, but after trimming and cooking there will be less to carve and serve. Pay attention to your weights and measures and recheck your arithmetic and none of your guests should go away hungry.

Liquid
1 cup=8 ounces
1 cup= 1/2 pint
2 cups=16 ounces
2 cups=1 pint
4 cups=32 ounces
4 cups=1 quart
8 cups=64 ounces
8 cups=2 quarts
8 cups=1/2 gallon
16 cups=128 ounces
16 cups=1 gallon
3 teaspoons=1 Tablespoon
4 Tablespoons=1/4 cup
16 Tablespoons=1 cup

Weights
1 pound=16 ounces
2 pounds=32 ounces
1/4 pound=4 ounces
1/2 pound=8 ounces
3/4 pound=12 ounces

Acknowledgements

I would like to take the time to thank the following people for use of the recipes, time, talent and for their friendship and support in the compilation of this book. Many hours went into the forming of the preceeding pages. Without the help of others it would not have come to fruition. My undying gratitude to you all. Thank you~ Bill.

At Morris Publishing, Heidi, for her patience and understanding.

To my family and friends: Joanne Hutcheson, Dianne Wood, Mary C. Tatum, Mother, Betty Stanley, Robin Dudley, Kate H. Tatum, Carol Freyne, June N. Spaulding (Nana), Aunt Ailene, Tinye Harding, Jeanie Smith, Nancy Howell, Les Spaulding, Mary Zacahry, Ray C. Watkins, Fred and Jen Shimalla, Bunnie Howell, Bonnie Zachary-Yurk, and foremost to God, for giving me the talent and ability to cook.

Index of Recipes

~*A*~

~ℬ~

Banana

Banana Pudding, Geneva's, 68
Banana Split Cake, Carol's, 97
Banana Walnut Ice Cream, 51

Beans

Baked Beans, 73
Fresh Green Beans, 26

Beef

Beef Filet, Bacon Wrapped, 164
Beef Stock, 221
Beef Tenderloin, Marinated, 108
Chili, Spicy, 137
Cocktail Meatballs, 179
Cold Roast Beef Sandwiches, 122
Hot Mexican Dip, 180

Beverages

Christmas Punch, 174
Grand Marnier Egg Nog, 175
Homemade Lemonade, 64
Ice Rings/Molds, 214
Plantation Tea Punch, 219
Tea Syrup, Julie Dwyer's 213

Blueberry

Blueberry Cheesecake Ice Cream, 50
Blueberry Congealed Salad, 24
Blueberry Muffins, Sister's, 21

Breads

Angel Biscuits, 206
Blueberry Muffins, Sister's, 21
Broccoli Cornbread, 140
Jalepeno Corn Muffins, 84

~*C*~

Cakes

Carrots

Casseroles

Cheesecake, Pumpkin, 131
Cheesestraws, Miss Fan's, 4
Curried Chutney Cheese, 179
Hot Mexican Dip, 180

Chocolate

Candy Bar Pie, 158
Cherry Chocolate Chip Ice Cream, 49
Chocolate Coconut Pie, 113
German Chocolate Brownies, 126
Praline Cake, 31
Stove Top Cookies, Ruth's, 198
White Chocolate Almond Ice Cream, 167
White Chocolate Ice Cream, 52

Coconut

Chocolate Coconut Pie, 113
Coconut Pie, Aunt Ailene's, 80
Japanese Fruitcake, 192
Japanese Fruitcake Icing, 193
Praline Cake, 31
Stove Top Cookies, Ruth's 198

Cookies

Bar:
Carol's Chewies, 127
German Chocolate Brownies, 126
Drop/Slice:
Almond Biscotti, Tinye's, 201
Ginger Crinkles, Jeanie's, 197
Refrigerator Cookies, 100
Sand Dollars, Milledge Street, 178
Sesame Thins, 184
Stove Top Cookie, Ruth's, 198
Sugar Cookies, Jeanie's, 199
Sugar Cookies, Ruth's, 200

Corn

Bourbon Corn Chowder, 139
Fresh Corn-Frozen Corn, 27
Grilled Corn on the Cob, 94

Crab

Crab and Red Pepper Bisque, 162
Crab Stew, Ann Parker's, 143
Crab Stuffed Mushrooms, 181
Crab Stuffed Potatoes, 166

Cranberry

Cranberry Congealed Salad, 188
Cranberry-Orange Relish, 176
Dried Cranberries with Walnuts Salad, 115

~ *D* ~

Desserts

Banana Pudding, Geneva's, 68
Bread Pudding with Whiskey Sauce, 119
Huguenot Tort, 132
Sauces:
Cinnamon Sauce, Dianne's, 149
Coffee Praline Sauce, 168
Raspberry Sauce, 112
Whiskey Sauce, 119

Dressings (Corn bread)

Corn bread Dressing with Giblet Gravy,
Mother's, 209
Oyster Dressing, 130
Sausage and Pecan Dressing, 129

~*E*~

Eggs

Breakfast Casserole, Miss Fan's, 19
Breakfast Casserole, Original, 157
Curried Egg Salad, 104
Chicken and Asparagus Quiche, 160
Deviled Eggs Supreme, Nana's, 67
Eggnog, Grand Marnier, 175
Sausage and Mushroom Quiche, 186

~*F*~

Fish

Catfish Fillets, Pecan Crusted, 82

Fruit

Ambrosia, 193
Fresh Fruit in a Grapefruit Bowl, 22
Midori Spiked Honeydew, 125

~*H*~

Ham

Bourbon-Brown Sugar Glazed Ham, 25
Dill Pickle and Ham Sandwhiches, 183
Ham Wrapped Asparagus, 182

~ *J* ~

Ice Cream

Banana Walnut Ice Cream, 51
Blueberry Cheesecake Ice Cream, 50
Cherry Chocolate Chip Ice Cream, 49
Lemon Ice Cream, 38
Lemon Sorbet, 86
Praline Ice Cream, Quick, 148
Straw-Ba-Nut Ice Cream, Robin Dudley's, 53
Vanilla Ice Cream, Basic, 207
White Chocolate Almond Ice Cream, 167
White Chocolate Ice Cream, 52

~ *J* ~

Jelly

Scuppernong Jelly, Mother's, 57

~ *L* ~

Lemon

Apricot Lemon Grilled Chicken, 41
Homemade Lemonade, 64
Lemon Buttermilk Sauce, Betty Stanley's, 96
Lemon Cheesecake, 111
Lemon Chess Pie, 17
Lemon Ice Cream, 38
Lemon Mustard BBQ Sauce, 211
Lemon Pecan Tart, 45

Lemon Sorbet, 86

~ *M* ~

Marinades
> Oriental Marinade, 107

Mushrooms
> Crab Stuffed Musrhooms, 181
> Creamy Turnip Green and Mushroom
> Soup, 116
> Creamy Wild Rice and Mushroom Soup, 138
> Sausage and Mushroom Quiche, 186

~ *N* ~

Nuts
> Brie with Almonds and Apricots, 103
> Cinnamon Sugar Pecans, 101
> Lemon Pecan Tart, 45
> Pecan Crusted Catfish Fillets, 82
> White Chocolate Almond Ice Cream, 167

~ *O* ~

Okra
> Carol's Pickled Okra, 59

Onions
> Creamy Leek and Potato Soup, 159
> Cucumber and Onion Salad, Jeanie's, 125

Onion Roasted Potatoes, 110

Orange
Cranberry Orange Relish, 176

Oyster
Oyster Dressing, 130
Oyster Pie, 190

~𝒫~

Peaches
Peach Preserves, Mother's, 60

Pears
Mixed Greens w/Pears and Walnuts, 163
Pear Preserves, Mother's, 4
Pear Relish, Mother's, 58

Pickles
Pickled Okra, Carol's, 59
Squash Pickle, Miss Kathleen's, 61

Pies
Candy Bar Pie, 158
Chocolate Coconut Pie, 113
Coconut Pie, Aunt Ailene's, 80
Lemon Chess Pie, 17
Peanut Butter Pie, Milledge Street, 98
Tartlet Dough, 216

Pork (see also Ham; Sausage)
Bavarian Pork Chops, 145
BBQ Pork Chops, 93
Pork Loin with Plum Sauce, 117
Spare Ribs, Spicy Bourbon Glazed, 79

Potatoes

Crab Stuffed Potatoes, 166
Creamy Leek and Potato Soup, 159
Onion Roasted Potatoes, 110
Potato Salad, June's Classic, 78
Potato Salad, Mother's, 65
Sweet Potatoes with Grand Marnier
and Pecan, 191
Sweet Potatoes, Mother's Candied, 28

Preserves

Peach Preserves, Mother's, 60
Pear Preserves, Mother's, 4

Puddings

Banana Pudding, Geneva's, 68
Bread Pudding with Whiskey Sauce, 119

~ *2* ~

Quiche

Chicken and Asparagus Quiche, 160
Sausage and Mushroom Quiche, 186

~ *R* ~

Relish

Chow Chow, Mama Kate's, 56
Cranberry Orange Relish, 176
Pear Relish, Mother's, 58
Squash Relish, 62

Rice

Creamy Wild Rice and Mushroom Soup, 138

Oriental Rice, 35
Rice continued~

Shrimp and Wild Rice Casserole, 109
Wild Rice Casserole, 44

~ *f* ~

Salads

Congealed:
Apricot Salad, Joanne's, 16
Blueberry Congealed Salad, 24
Cranberry Salad, 188
Lime Buttermilk Salad, 33
Pretzel Salad, Great Pee Dee, 71
Raspberry Congealed Salad,
Betty Stanley's, 151
Fruit:
Ambrosia, 193
Dried Cranberries with Walnuts Salad, 115
Fresh Fruit in a Grapefruit Bowl, 22
Honeydew, Midori Spiked, 125
Mixed Green with Pears and Walnuts, 163
Meat & Egg:
Curried Egg Salad, 104
Gourmet Chicken Salad, Marianne's, 15
Shrimp Salad, Milledge House, 123
Slaw:
Marinated Slaw with Red Peppers, 85
Nana's Slaw, 66
Pasta:
Milledge House Pasta Salad, 95

Vegetable:
Baby Marinated Carrots, 124
Bitter Winter Salad, 144
Caesar Salad, 40
Cucumber and Onion Salad, Jeanie's, 125
Mixed Greens with Pears and Walnuts, 163
Potato Salad, June's Classic, 78
Potato Salad, Mother's, 65
Seven Layer Salad, 70
Tossed Salad Greens, 208

Salad Dressings
Blue Cheese Dressing, Milledge Street, 107
Easy Vinaigrette, 144
Lemon Buttermilk Sauce, Betty Stanley's, 96
Red Wine Vinaigrette, 115
Tarragon Vinaigrette, 208

Sandwiches
Cold Roast Beef Sandwiches, 122
Cool Chicken Cordon Blue Sandwiches, 121
Dill Pickle and Ham Sandwiches, 183

Sauces
Savory:
BBQ Sauce, Betty Stanley's, 77
Giblet Gravy, 210
Lemon Mustard BBQ Sauce, 211
Lime Cilantro Mayonnaise, 82
Oriental Marinade, 107
Plum Sauce, 117
Sweet:
Cinnamon Sauce, Dianne's, 149
Coffee Praline Sauce, 168
Lemon Buttermilk Sauce, Betty Stanley's, 96

Raspberry Sauce, 11
Whiskey Sauce, 119

Sausage

Breakfast Casserole, Miss Fan's, 19
Breakfast Casserole, Original, 157
Hot Chicken and Sausage Dip, 180
Sausage and Mushroom Quiche, 186
Sausage and Pecan Dressing, 129

Seafood

Crab:

Crab and Red Pepper Bisque, 162
Crab Stew, Ann Parker's, 143
Crab Stuffed Mushrooms, 181
Crab Stuffed Potatoes, 166

Shrimp:

Pickled Shrimp, 102
Shrimp Dip, 177
Shrimp Salad, Milledge House, 123
Shrimp and Wild Rice Casserole, 109

Oyster:

Oyster Dressing, 130
Oyster Pie, 190

Soups

Bourbon Corn Chowder, 139
Brunswick Stew, Hugh and J.W.'s, 75
Chili, Spicy, 137
Crab and Red Pepper Bisque, 162
Crab Stew, Ann Parker's, 143
Creamy Leek and Potato Soup, 159
Creamy Turnip Green and Mushroom
Soup, 116
Creamy Wild Rice and Mushroom Soup, 138

Squash

Baked Squash, 42
Carolina Baked Vegetables, 155
Squash Casserole, Milledge House, 156
Squash Pickle, Miss Kathleen's, 61
Squash Relish, 62
Squash Sauteed with Dill, 146

Stews

Brunswick Stew, Hugh and J.W.'s, 75
Crab Stew, Ann Parker's, 143

~ *T* ~

Tomatoes

Broiled Herbed Tomatoes, 153
Canned Tomatoes, Carol's, 55
Grilled Tomatoes, 43
Tomatoes Stuffed with Grits and Greens, 83

Turkey

Deep Fried Turkey, 72
Turkey Roasted with Herbs, 189
Turkey Roasting Timetable, 128

Turnip Greens

Creamy Turnip Green and Musrhoom
Soup, 116
Tomatoes Stuffed with Grits and Greens, 83
Turnip Greens, 216

~ *V* ~

Vegetables

Carolina Baked Vegetables, 155
Mixed Grilled Vegetables, 165

About the Author

William E. Coxwell is a 1989 graduate of Johnson and Wales University of Charleston, South Carolina where he earned a degree in Culinary Arts. He plans to start his own gourmet food line and is currently at work on a Christmas cookbook available autumn 2001. He is also the author of *The Coxwell Collection.*

Order Form

Southern Menus for Entertaining
By William E. Coxwell
P.O. Box 148
Appling, Georgia 30802

Send me ____copies of Southern Menus @ $16.95 each_____
Shipping and Handling $3.00_____
Total amount enclosed_____

(Please make checks payable to William Coxwell)